Parenting has never been more challenging, and our team at Focus on the Family hears regularly from moms and dads who are pulling their hair out in an effort to raise godly, responsible children. In this wise and insightful volume, Dr. Kathy Koch has reminded parents how important it is to build our parenting on a foundation of solid, loving bonds with our kids. When we start there, our discipline, correction, and training are much more likely to reach our children's hearts.

JIM DALY
President, Focus on the Family

In an age when parents are being challenged to take a back seat to the culture, struggling with opposing ideologies and an ever-changing social landscape, Dr. Kathy Koch is a much-needed voice of reassurance, biblical wisdom, and strength. How do we reach the heart of our kids? How do I help my child find his identity and purpose? How do I transition with my child into the teen years successfully? The answer, of course, lies in the heart. When giving up is easier, Dr. Kathy gently reminds us why we must never give up. Parenting is faith work at every stage, but with a little help from Kathy, you will gain confidence. *Start with the Heart* is a must-read book for every parent!

HEIDI ST. JOHN
Author of *Becoming MomStrong and Prayers for the Battlefield*
Founder of MomStrongInternational.com

Dr. Kathy has done it again. As parents of four, my wife and I have benefited from every book she's written, and this is no exception. She's a wise guide, a coach who helps keep our parenting priorities straight as we seek to walk with our children into a life full of loving God and others as He created them to do.

JOHN STONESTREET
President of the Colson Center and author of *A Practical Guide to Culture*

We cannot stress enough how important this book will be to your goal of becoming a good parent. Dr. Kathy Koch brilliantly weaves her core principles throughout these pages—principles that have literally revolutionized the way we view our kids and ourselves. *Start with the Heart* will not only inspire you to be a better parent but will equip you with the tools you need to succeed. We couldn't put it down!

DAVID AND JASON BENHAM
Nationally acclaimed entrepreneurs, authors, speakers

It's shocking how fragile so many young adults are these days. They're afraid of failure and unwilling to take risks. They scurry for safe spaces on campus because they can't bear to encounter challenging ideas. What young adults need most today is *resilience*, and that's why *Start with the Heart* is so refreshing. It's page after page of practical ideas from real families that show how to rise above the challenges of our age to raise secure, brave kids. Thank you Dr. Kathy!

JEFF MYERS
President, Summit Ministries, and author of *The Secret Battle of Ideas about God*

Most parents hope to raise compassionate, courageous, and responsible kids, yet many are at a loss as to how that can be done. Dr. Kathy Koch clearly coaches and gently guides the well-intentioned mom and dad to interact and connect with their child in a way that builds relationship while growing godly character. She unpacks her "start with the heart" philosophy with practical and easily applicable strategies so the parent is not left wondering, "How do I apply this?" The entire family will be blessed and strengthened by the principles and positive practices presented in this powerful parenting book.

LORI WILDENBERG
Speaker and author of five parenting books, including *The Messy Life of Parenting*

We all want to help our children move from "obeying" to being internally motivated to do what's right. But we can be clueless on *how* to do that! In this book, you'll learn from the master—in an easy-to-understand, super-practical format. I greatly admire Dr. Kathy Koch's ability to present profound concepts in a simple way that helps us immediately. And once you read this book, you will too.

SHAUNTI FELDHAHN
International speaker and bestselling author of *For Women Only* and *The Kindness Challenge*

Parents who love their child will find actionable insight in Dr. Koch's book *Start with the Heart*. Her emphases on biblical truth, the importance of understanding the needs all of us have, communication, honesty, and compassion are great foundations for any family. The older teens and young adults we serve who face confusing and difficult challenges in life might not be in these situations today if they had lived their childhood in the environment described in *Start with the Heart*. Read this book! Then DO this book! You'll see! Your children's change is born in your own change! Your expanded ability to parent will surprise you! Just follow the simple directions! Be brave! Trust God to pave your way and your child's path as well. Start with your heart!

MARY MARGARET GIBSON
Ministry Director, Save the Mother, Save Her Child–EvanTell, Inc.

In this screen-driven world, the heart is often overlooked. *Start with the Heart* defines what's truly important in parenting. Dr. Kathy Koch is a gifted communicator with both kids and parents. Put the sample conversations in this book to use, then get ready for positive transformation in your heart and home.

ARLENE PELLICANE
Speaker and author of *Parents Rising*

Do you want to stop nagging and move your children from "I can't" and "I won't," to "I can, I will, and I did?" If your answer is yes, the words on these pages will equip you like no other book. I have learned so much from Dr. Kathy Koch and I know you will too!

JILL SAVAGE
Author of *No More Perfect Moms and Real Moms . . . Real Jesus*

In *Start with the Heart*, Dr. Kathy shares sound biblical principles and practical applications in easy-to-read chapters. Whether you are a parent of littles, middles, or older children, Dr. Kathy will help you understand how to motivate your children and become the parent they need. The ideas can change your relationship with your children because you'll stop trying to change their outward behavior by focusing on their hearts for long-lasting change.

CONNIE ALBERS
Speaker and author of *Parenting beyond the Rules*

Start with the Heart is an incredible resource, and such an important book for parents. It's an easy read that is chock-full of wisdom and practical, simple application. Though our children are now grown, I can tell you—they'll all be receiving a copy of this powerful book from Mary Jo and me for use as a *go-to resource* in raising our grandchildren.

BRENNAN DEAN
President, Great Homeschool Conventions, Inc.

Dr. Kathy Koch has written a must-read for parenting a generation that is at risk of becoming detached and indifferent. As a child development specialist, I believe we are in a crisis when it comes to our young teens and their view of life and themselves. What we are teaching them through social media isn't working. If parents read this book and implement its contents, lives could be changed and, I dare say, saved. This powerful book will inform, empower, and provide guidance needed to raise independent, loving, and well-adjusted children.

KATHY LEE EGGERS
Child development specialist, author, and speaker

Every homeschooling parent I know wants to motivate his or her children to do well in life—academically, relationally, and spiritually. These precious moms and dads love their children more than anything but sometimes lack self-confidence or need help to learn and apply realistic, practical parenting strategies. *Start with the Heart* is just what they need! In it, Kathy realistically acknowledges the challenges parents face but doesn't stay there. Instead, she then details how we can overcome those difficulties, provides specific and reasonable ideas for how to make improvements, and cheers us along on the journey. I urge every homeschooling parent to read and work through *Start with the Heart*.

TINA HOLLENBECK
Founder of The Homeschool Resource Roadmap

Kathy Koch has done it again. In her encouraging and practical style, she has written a book that will set parents into action, chasing after the hearts of their children so they, in turn, will pursue the heart of God. I found myself learning and nodding in agreement on every page. This is what we need as we raise kids who will shine the light of Jesus in this generation. *Start with the Heart* is a guidebook that will help you diligently tend the hearts of your children from a place of love.

LEE NIENHUIS
Communications specialist for Moms in Prayer International, speaker, Bible teacher, author of *Brave Moms, Brave Kids*, farm wife, busy mom, and host of the Moms in Prayer Podcast

Start with the Heart is a powerful book on faith-based attachment parenting. Dr. Koch as usual packs tremendous content in concise words. I'm working through her fabulous list from chapter 1 because I know if I'm successful, my children have a greater chance of being so also. I'm grateful that *Start with the Heart* challenges me as a professional counselor and parent of two to intentionally create spiritually motivated heart connections with our kids.

MICHELLE NIETERT
Licensed Professional Counselor Supervisor, Clinical Director of Community Counseling Associates

Dads—please read this book. (Moms, you can read it, too.) No doubt, we want our kids to do well and we set high standards. But sometimes, to our kids, our critique sounds more like criticism, especially when we only point out how they came up short and don't talk about their strengths. If this is your norm, Dr. Kathy can help you change . . . before it's too late.

ROLAND C. WARREN
President and CEO of Care Net and author of *Bad Dads of the Bible*

Parents are struggling to connect with their children like never before. With anxiety, depression, and suicide in children and teens at an all-time high, families need to be strong and parents and children need to be deeply connected. Kathy Koch shares wisdom and practical application for parents as they navigate parenthood and establish heart connections with their children. Winsome analogies bring the God-given roles and responsibilities of parenting to life while relevant questions help parents honestly reflect. No matter the state or phase of your family, *Start with the Heart* will help you lay, build, restore, or solidify stronger relationships within the home, reach the heart of your children, and impact their heart motivations for good.

SUZANNE PHILLIPS
Cofounder of Hearts at Home 2.0 and Legacy Community Academy, Alpharetta, GA

All too often books for parents focus on performance over substance. In our search for answers on how to parent well, we allow ourselves to settle for the quick fixes instead of committing to the work of deep transformation within ourselves and with our children. Dr. Koch offers us an invitation to pursue transformation.

SUSAN SEAY
International speaker, author, and host of the Mentor 4 Moms Podcast

What I deeply adore about the new book *Start with the Heart* is that is Dr. Kathy's wisdom and compassion poured out on the page for all of us parents who have done all the "trying harder" we can and have come to the end of ourselves. It is a release from "just do more" parenting and calls us instead to learn to love more fully and deeply with a heart open wide. It's about learning deep compassion not just for your child but for yourself as a flawed human learning to parent fearlessly. What a freeing book! Could not recommend highly enough.

KATHI LIPP
Bestselling author of *The Husband Project* and *Clutter Free*

START
WITH THE
HEART

How to Motivate Your Kids to Be
Compassionate, Responsible, and Brave
(Even When You're Not Around)

KATHY KOCH, PhD

MOODY PUBLISHERS
CHICAGO

Scripture quotations are from The Holy Bible, English Standard Version® (ESV®), copyright © 2001, 2007 by Crossway, a publishing ministry of Good News Publishers. Used by permission. All rights reserved.

Edited by Elizabeth Cody Newenhuyse
Interior design: Ragont Design and Erik M. Peterson
Cover design: Erik M. Peterson
Cover illustration of heart copyright © 2018 by best4u/Shutterstock (284283518). All rights reserved.

ISBN: 978-0-8024-1885-2

We hope you enjoy this book from Moody Publishers. Our goal is to provide high-quality, thought-provoking books and products that connect truth to your real needs and challenges. For more information on other books and products that will help you with all your important relationships, go to www.moodypublishers.com or write to:

Moody Publishers
820 N. La Salle Boulevard
Chicago, IL 60610

1 3 5 7 9 10 8 6 4 2

Printed in the United States of America

I dedicate this book to my prayer warriors who support me consistently and practically. I'm grateful for their faith.

I regularly prayed Psalm 90:17 over this project and their support and God's favor resulted in many, many "yeses." God motivates me and so do they.

Let the favor of the Lord our God be upon us,
and establish the work of our hands upon us;
yes, establish the work of our hands!

Contents

Foreword

A year ago, my wife and I started on a journey. As parents of six children who are trying to raise our kids to embrace biblical values, we know it can sometimes feel like the entire world is working against us. The digital age is increasingly filling our children with wrong worldviews, distractions, anxiety, and loneliness. With social media outlets, movies, video games, music, and celebrities telling our children what they should believe—about themselves, God, family, politics, and morality—the job of a parent to successfully guide their children can seem like a losing battle. Chelsea and I were committed to finding new ways to stay connected with our children in an *antisocial* media world. We wanted our kids to champion healthy technology habits that would lead to their success. We wanted to teach them how to be connected online but not disconnected in the *real world*. This led us to create a film called *Connect*.

In my search for guidance, I interviewed Dr. Kathy Koch for the film. Kathy was a treasure trove of wisdom! She identified so many cultural lies being taught to our kids and their corresponding biblical truths. She brought Scripture to life through her colorful lessons. Kathy taught me that by encouraging humility, compassion, bravery, and perseverance in our children, we are equipping them to make right decisions that will carry them to good places in the future. And now, thanks to the principles in her new book, *Start with the Heart*, I have even more tools to help me better understand, communicate with, and model for my children the kind of qualities I want to see in them.

As you learn from Kathy Koch how to guide, comfort, and encourage your children, I hope you will commit to seeking your child's heart; it's the only way to have a real and lasting impact. I hope you feel as encouraged as I did by the exercises and reflection points she provides at the end of each chapter.

I am writing this in a hotel room after my family and I were evacuated from wildfires raging toward our home. In this instance, where I could lose everything of material value, I am reminded how blessed I am to have the love of God, my family, and the hearts of my children. That is all I need.

KIRK CAMERON

Relationships Rule

"No, you can't have an Instagram account. We've told you this 1,000 times! You're too young, you don't need it, and we want you to value your friends face-to-face. We've told you! Don't ask again. *We'll* decide if and when you can have one and no amount of asking on your part will influence us."

Why is this preteen demanding something from her parents when they've told her "no" before? What do you think they are doing or not doing?

"I told you to put away your toys and you're still playing with them? What's up with that? You know better! Put them away. NOW!"

How do you think this parent and child got to this point? What's gone wrong?

"What do you mean you can't memorize this week's vocabulary definitions? You didn't have any trouble memorizing them last week or the week before. Stop complaining! And don't ask for a prize when you do learn them. You've shown me you don't need one. Just get it done! Be diligent!"

What did this parent do right? What could this parent have done differently?

Are any of these scenarios familiar to you? Parenting isn't for the faint of heart. I'm proud of every parent who is intent on parenting well and doing it on the good days and bad. This is you! I know that's true because you're interested in how to motivate your children. You're not satisfied with how things are going; you're leaning in. You want something more for them. For yourself.

The "Why" of Your Relationship with Your Kids

Capturing your child's heart and parenting to keep it may be more important than anything else you do. Your love for your children and your desire for them to trust Christ for their salvation matters greatly. For you to have motivational power to help them make that commitment, mature in their faith, and love God more fully, you must start with their heart.

For your children to want what you want for them, for changes to occur, and for improvements to remain, your hearts must be intertwined. Your motivational power and influence over their obedience comes out of the love you have for each other. This is certainly true when thinking about motivating children. No matter your concerns that surround motivating your kids—moving them from apathy to action, disrespect to respect, self-centeredness to compassion, getting Cs to earning As—you must start with their heart.

Caring more about the quality of your relationship than the quality of children's behavior allows you to affect their behavior. In contrast, when children think their behavior matters more than anything, they will care less what you think. Your impact will decrease. Prioritizing your relationship is everything. It makes you influential in your own family.

My son, give me your heart, and let your eyes observe my ways.
—Proverbs 23:26

How would you describe the value of your relationship with your children? Facebook friends explained it this way:

My relationship with my daughter will impact her for the rest of her life. It will be how she sees God, other adults, and even the world. If I have a negative relationship with my daughter where I tear her down and she can never do anything right, then that will be how she sees herself in the future. However, if I have a positive and open relationship with my daughter, she will have confidence, she will be more willing to accept God, and she will have a more positive view of the world and others. Not to mention, I want her to be able to talk to me when she grows up. I want to know if something is wrong at school, with friends, etc. I want her to ask me for advice rather than asking the world for advice because I will point her to God while the world will point her to other things. —Victoria

My relationship with my children matters because all of the other things I do with my life will pass away, but the love and guidance I pour into my children will influence them and generations to come. It is the most important legacy I can leave. —Dawn

A strong, trust-based relationship with my children matters because the world sings a different song to them daily about their identity and their place in this world. —Laura

Without relationship, there is no true respect, obedience, or honesty. There is nothing to bridge the generation gap. Just as God first draws us in with a relationship, that

then stirs a desire within us to seek Him for guidance and obey His commands, we must focus on building an authentic relationship with our children if we ever want more than performance-based obedience. If our desire is mutual love and respect and eventual friendship, we have to start building that foundation when they're children.
—Hannah

Again I ask, how would you describe the value of your relationship with your children? Why do your children matter, and why does your connection to each other matter? How might your children answer these questions?

I predict your relationship with your children matters greatly to you. Think back over the past week or so with each child in mind. What's the evidence that your relationship matters greatly? Think about how you spent your time, talent, and other resources. How did you pray? Did you explore ideas together and have fun together? Did you talk with them about their friends, struggles, successes, and plans? How did you put your belief that the relationship matters into practice?

The "How" of Your Relationship with Your Kids

You can establish and maintain a quality relationship with your children. It's the prerequisite to all the ideas I present in the book. Without them knowing their heart is safe with you, they may not listen. They may not believe you. They may not care what you think. They may not want to achieve the goals you have for them. Your compliments and corrections may fall on deaf ears.

The word *parent* has Latin roots and means "to bring forth." You'll bring forth much that is positive when you have a vibrant, growing give-and-take relationship with your children. Start with their heart in mind. Parent so the Lord's love captures their hearts. End with their heart in mind. You must.

My friend Michael spends one-on-one time with each of his three young daughters regularly. He makes them a priority, and they know it. He has a fulltime job, is studying to earn his DMin, volunteers in their church, is an entrepreneur, and serves several nonprofits with his unique skill set. He's busy! He chooses to not let his tasks rob him of his relationships. His wife does the same thing. (There's really no such thing as not having enough time. It's all about what we do with the time we have.)

My friends Tina and Jeff prioritize their teen daughters and they always have. They each spend one-on-one time with them. When the girls were young, they both participated in the same activities—ballet, piano lessons, camping, and more. Now the girls are secure because they are known by their parents and allowed to prioritize the talents and relationships that matter to them. They also all serve together at church, but in different activities that suite their interests and abilities. Rachel and Abbie are individuals in a tight family unit.

Suzanne and Lane prioritize their three teens and their teens' friends. Not only do Ward, Lilly, and Ansley know they matter to their parents, but their friends know they matter. They're welcome in their home, and they're fed in their home— often! Also, when Lane and Suzanne visit Ward and Ansley in college and go out to dinner, they make sure to invite their friends to join them. They want to know who their children are being influenced by. And Ward and Ansley want their friends to know their parents. Prioritizing their children's friends has solidified their family bond. Their children want to be home and want to be with them.

I pray you're in a good place with your kids. No matter how things are going now, your relationship can be healthier than it is. If you'd score it a B, let's make it an A. If it's currently a C, let's find out what would make it a B and then observe to see if it can become an A, especially by implementing ideas in this book.

> **Being understood is evidence of love.**

The ideas will work if you prioritize your children's hearts so they know you love them, know them, and understand them. Every child wants and needs to be known; being invisible is painful. Being understood is evidence of love. Note how I worded this. It's not enough for you to know them, understand them, and love them. *They* need to know.

Tedd Tripp's statement is motivational, especially if you're raising teens:

> Pressures of the teen years pull children away from home. This is the time when they develop comradery with those who "understand them." They are looking for relationships in which someone knows, understands and loves them. Your children should not have to leave home for that. You can provide family relationships in which your children are understood and embraced.[1]

My friend Lori Wildenberg also understands the value of starting with the heart. Do you want for your children what she wants for hers? She writes, "A great and godly parenting strategy is relational. I want to interact with my kids in a way that deepens our relationship, encourages responsibility, draws grace into the family fold, and molds a humble countenance."[2]

Sometimes we complicate things. Yes, parenting is multifaceted, and our children and we are complex. People can be messy, and our culture is chaotic. Hopelessness is not appropriate. Hope is. Not everything is as hard as we think it is.

Securing Their Hearts

Here's my list of understandings that can secure children's hearts and increase your influence so you'll be able to motivate them to be responsible, brave, compassionate, and so much more. Ideas in the chapters that follow support and build upon these truths.

- Parent by faith. Pray for God's insight and direction, let Him work in your child, and trust Him with the result while you parent with thoughtful intentionality.

- Parent with grace and mercy. Although consistently responding to children's behavior is important, so is surprising them with your kindness. Know when they're willfully disobedient and when they're not.

- Forgive quickly and often. Ask to be forgiven quickly and often. Remember that the past does not define your children or control the future.

- Tell your children you are confident in God. Teach them Scripture, pray for and with them, go to church together, and serve with them.

- Prioritize children, not their behavior.

- You can dislike what children *do* while you still like and love them. Remember we can all have bad days.

- Be who you want your children to be. And teach them who you want them to be. Much is caught *and* taught. Want them to be successful.

- Children are human beings, not human doings. Who they are is more important than what they do.

- Raise the children you were given, not the children you wish you had.

- Create memories and build traditions with individual children and with your family. Laugh, dream, think, feel, play, read, and explore together.

- Parent so children will want to be your friend later. Don't prioritize friendship now.

- Remember needs and wants are different. Children don't need everything they want. Parent to meet their needs.

- Seek to understand before trying to be understood. Ask better questions. Listen longer. Be fully present without devices in your hands.

- Listen when children are little if you want them to talk with you when they're older. Answer their questions when they're little if you want them to ask questions when they're older.

- When children have a problem, remember they are not the problem. Help them without making them feel like a project you're trying to finish or a problem you're trying to solve.

- Teach children to fail well. Life can be challenging. They must be able to recover from adversity.

- Unconditionally love and value your children. Ideally, there's nothing they can do that would cause you to love them more *or* less. They should not have to prove their value to you.

- Prioritize progress, not perfection. Remember, you and your children are being perfected, but Jesus is the only One who is perfect. Perfection is the destination; transformation is how our children and we will get there.

I hope this list is both encouraging and challenging. Ideas in the chapters that follow support and build upon these truths. Would you agree that relationship changes are easier to make when everyone knows about the new goals and expectations? Children sometimes tell me, "I feel like my parents have the rule book. I wish they'd share it with me." Perhaps this list can serve as a rule book of sorts.

Is Your Child Resilient?

The more I studied and prepared to write this book, the more I became convinced that resiliency might be the most important quality for motivated children to have. Every child will experience times of struggle, pain, and loss. Work may be hard, school can be challenging, and chores may be boring. People—even parents—may treat them unfairly. People might lie to them and they may feel left out at times. They may be bullied.

But resiliency is the ability to recover quickly from adversity, disappointment, defeat, failure, and trauma. It's an essential ability if your children are going to be motivated by you and what you do. It's essential if you want them to develop self-motivation. It offers protection against anxiety and becoming depressed.[3]

Resilient children will "still experience anger, grief and pain, but [are] able to keep functioning—both physically and psychologically." Children who lack resilience "might dwell on problems, feel victimized, become overwhelmed or turn to unhealthy coping mechanisms, such as substance abuse."[4]

Resilient children aren't victims. They're survivors. They know challenges are a part of life and necessary for growth. They are not defined by them. They are motivated by them and learn from them. Their ability to stay strong, not stay down, and come through challenging experiences and adversity in one piece is what resiliency is all about. They bounce back from setbacks. Comebacks are a strength. Resiliency starts as a choice when children are acquiring this ability. With experience, it becomes a part of who they are.[5]

These children can rebound from disappointments more quickly than others because they rely on inner strengths and they reach out to you and possibly others for comfort and instruction. Being able to reach out to others for support is a key component of being resilient.[6] Resilient children ask for help

> **Become more aware of how resilient you are.**

because they value themselves and their task, and they believe they can be effective and will be effective. This is called *self-efficacy*, and it's related to resiliency. It has also been identified as a thrive skill. Self-efficacy protects children from learned helplessness and the Eeyore-like characteristics shared by passive pessimists.[7]

The toys in the classic children's book *The Little Engine That Could* are a true example of especially this characteristic of resiliency. We always think of the little engine bravely saying, "I think I can," but the toys, bound for children on Christmas, showed resiliency in searching for a train that would take them where they were going. They bounced back from failure and got on with it. One agreed to help. The toys didn't give up. Your children (and you) need to be resilient like they were.

Become more aware of how resilient you are. Your children are watching how you respond when in a valley. Talk with them about your attitudes, behaviors, thoughts, and feelings as they relate to failing. Talk about theirs. Other ideas in later chapters will give you further help in developing this important quality.

Resiliency will develop when you start with children's hearts and prioritize your relationship. I pray you're hopeful and eager to see what the future holds. Be resilient—children who have been sitting down in their valleys lately will need to learn to stand up and walk forward. With your encouragement and teaching, they will.

WHAT ABOUT YOU?

Do you remember the relationship you had—or didn't have—with your parents? Maybe they modeled what relationships looked like more than taught about them. Or, perhaps they taught about them, but didn't live them out. The generation of kids you're raising is different in so many ways. Yet the truths are still the same. Ask your kids how important it is for them to have a good relationship with you. Then tell them what it means to you.

THINGS TO DO

- Because knowing and understanding your children is so important for the quality of your relationship, grab a piece of paper for each of your kids. Make a list of what you know about them. Think about all their years and their likes, wants, and needs. Think about what they do and who they are. Consider their thoughts and feelings. Think about their strengths, challenges, abilities, and hobbies. Think in terms of people and tasks. Have the paper handy and keep adding to it as you observe and interact with your child. When you're ready, sit down with your child and share your lists. They'll be encouraged and probably enjoy adding things you didn't think of.

- Have your children ask several people of different ages to share about a mistake they made and what they learned from it. Share your stories, too. Ask your children what they learned from the interviews.

- As a family, choose to learn something new. You could go miniature golfing or bowling if all your children are inexperienced. You could learn to make balloon animals, juggle, or practice calligraphy. Acknowledge that learning new things can be frustrating. Keep track of efforts, acknowledge feelings, don't give up, and celebrate when progress is made. Doing this on a somewhat regular basis can help you and your children become more resilient.[8]

THINGS TO THINK ABOUT

- How did you react to my recommendations for how to secure children's hearts and increase your influence? Did you mark the ones you want to think more about and work on? Which ones helped you feel good about how you've been doing? Are there any you want to talk with your spouse or children about?

- Think of a time in your life when you needed to be resilient. How did you do? Did you get stuck or were you able to bounce back? Can you share this with your children when the time is right?

I believe that appreciation is a holy thing,
that when we look for what's best in the
person we happen to be with at the moment,
we're doing what God does. So, in loving
and appreciating our neighbor, we're
participating in something truly sacred.

FRED ROGERS

Host of *Mister Rogers' Neighborhood*,

in a commencement address at Marquette University, 2001[9]

Character:
A Skill and A Will

Starting with the heart and working to establish and maintain a healthy relationship with your children makes it more likely you'll be able to influence their heart. This matters greatly because the heart is the wellspring of all life.

> *Above all else, guard your heart,*
> *for everything you do flows from it.*
> —PROVERBS 4:23

God's Word doesn't declare the mind to be the wellspring of life. And God's Word doesn't declare the heart to be the wellspring of behavior. No—all of *life* springs from the *heart*. Of course, this doesn't mean the mind is irrelevant. Let's remember that we are called to "love the Lord your God with all your heart and with all your soul and with all your mind and with all your strength" (Mark 12:30).

And at the heart of motivating your child is that important word *character*.

This is not always a word we think of in connection with children. We think of character in business, politics, and church leadership. But think about the motivation struggles you're having lately with one or more of your children. Is your youngest not following through with chores, so you have to follow her around constantly? Is your middle son teasing his younger brother, even though you've threatened him to get him to stop? Is your oldest bored by school and satisfied with poor daily work? Are two of your kids obsessed with an online game and ignoring siblings and letting schoolwork slide?

Do you see how character is a factor? It's central to their decisions. Their character affects attitudes and abilities. Which traits they use and which they don't use are thought about in their minds and felt in their hearts. Character is both a skill and a will. Children need to know what to do *and* be willing to behave in that way.

When your children frustrate you, you can gain cause-effect confidence to determine the causes. Is it impatience causing no effort today? Or is it fear? Jealousy resulting in bullying a brother? Or anger? A need for control preventing your daughter from trying something new? Or is it perfectionism? Desire for happiness causing complaining? Or is it an authority issue? Why aren't they motivated like you want them to be?

Building a Better Character So Motivation Lasts

Our character informs our behavior. That's true both for children and for us adults. For example, because children are patient, they behave a certain way. Patient children (and grown-ups) wait in line without complaining. Patient children wait while a sibling or friend gets a drink from their mom or dad.

Our kids will encounter uphill battles that make the future hard to see: detours on the way to meet their goals, potholes that slow them down, and barriers to their plans. Or dare I mention no cell signal or a lost phone?! It's godly character that will get them through. It's what can be consistent no matter the path they're on and whether we're with them or not. This is why motivating your children's hearts for what's right pays a greater dividend than emphasizing right behavior.

Without Christlike character, implementing ideas to improve motivation is like putting a Band-Aid on a gushing wound. Even the best ideas implemented faithfully will not result in consistent positive change if their character is not transformed. Transformation happens as character is caught and taught. Be alert to *your* character and to teachable moments from your life and your children's. Take advantage of them.

Whoever walks with the wise becomes wise,
but the companion of fools will suffer harm.
—PROVERBS 13:20

Also, affirm your children when they do use the character qualities you're emphasizing and correct them when they don't. (See chapter 9 for ideas about how to do this well.) Compliments and corrections can help children make necessary changes that result in consistent character and consistent motivation.

> Be alert to your character and to teachable moments from your life.

For each of the character qualities you choose to prioritize, think about whether you and your children exhibit it consistently. If not, observe to discern why you don't. Is there a pattern to the problem? What's in the way? Relationship conflicts? A long-lasting habit? Laziness? Another sin? Lack of role modeling? Too much yelling and not enough teaching? Identifying a reason may help you and your children make changes so the character quality becomes a part of their identity and yours. (You'll learn a reliable process to help you in the next chapter.)

Specifically, look for *gratitude* and *joy*. The lack of one or both of these emotions causes children (and adults) to use character qualities inconsistently. When parents prioritize consistent joy, and not circumstantial happiness, and consistent gratitude, and not circumstantial thankfulness, children are more likely to especially respect themselves and others and be self-controlled.[1] Ask yourself if your children think gratitude and joy are important to you. Ask yourself.

Because Christlike character isn't easy, we can't just talk about the qualities or depend on teachable moments. We need to teach to the mind and the heart. We need to make sure children *know* that something is right or wrong and also help them to *feel* whether it is right or wrong. And, as you'll learn more about in chapter 6, you can also coach your children to be of sound character, cheer for them, and be a referee, as needed. Sticking with the process will result in the product you want.

You know what causes teaching about character qualities to fall on deaf ears? Hypocrisy. Think about your life. If the people around you aren't kind, brave, and humble, but they want you to be, it's harder for you, right? Also, if I'm tired, in a bad mood, overwhelmed, or self-centered, it's easy for my character to fail me.

Children are even more susceptible to the influences around them. We should have and model solid character so our behavior, attitudes, and decisions glorify God. We should also prioritize our character so we don't lead a child astray. Making every effort to use the qualities ourselves matters. And, of course, apologizing when we don't is key to maintaining a positive relationship.

I want us to rise above our circumstances, stop blaming

our past, and choose to develop the character qualities that lead to health and life. If we don't, our children most likely won't. This lack of resiliency (as we have seen) can be among the reasons motivation is weak and misdirected. There are reasons our character may falter at times. But as you'll want to tell your children, "reasons" aren't excuses for poor behavior.

Character Qualities: What's Most Important?

Although we could make a case that every character quality is related to motivation, I'll highlight a few here that are especially relevant—for your children *and* you. You can personalize this by looking at the list in Appendix A, possibly with your children, and choosing other qualities that relate to your family values and climate or to one or more of your children.[2] (For example, joy might be needed if a child constantly complains. Cooperation will be helpful if children aren't motivated to play or work well together.) Also, suggestions about teaching the character qualities are on the book's website: www.StartWith TheHeart.net. Some guidelines for different ages are included.

Because I believe some character qualities especially affect others, I've listed them in a particular order. Think about their cause-effect relationships as you read. Consider these qualities:

Humble

I agree with psychologist and author Thomas Lickona who

writes that "humility motivates us to try to become better people."[3] It gives birth to the choice to exhibit other character traits.

Humble children can admit they don't know everything. They're teachable and not proud or arrogant. They won't panic or quickly give up when something is challenging. They believe they can learn, so they listen more intently, take your direction, and are more likely to improve. Humble children usually argue less and more readily submit to authority. Also, they don't need to show off and let others know they did something better than them. Humility positively affects relationships.

Parents need this quality, too. Trying to parent children without being humble is dangerous. Without humility, parents may pass the buck and blame others when things don't go well. They may strive for perfection because anything other than that makes them uncomfortable. Pride can cause parents to bully their children into being who they need them to be.

Before destruction a man's heart is haughty,
but humility comes before honor.
—PROVERBS 18:12

Self-respect

When children have a proper understanding of their value, they will be more motivated to acquire positive character qualities, be obedient, and accomplish much. When they don't value themselves, they don't need to be good or positive about anything. Teaching children principles like God created them in His image (Genesis 1:27), for His glory (Isaiah 43:7), and gifted them in advance to do good works (Ephesians 2:10) establishes a self-understanding and self-respect that makes other character qualities necessary and desirable. So does treating them with respect. If you don't respect them, why would they respect themselves?

Parents who respect themselves will work to develop the necessary knowledge to parent well. They'll stand up for themselves and not be open to children's manipulation. They'll ask for help when they need it and follow through on what they learn.

So God created man in his own image, in the image
of God he created him; male and female he created them.
—Genesis 1:27

Self-control

Children with self-control think, feel, and act in ways that line up with their values and benefit others. Their impulses don't control them. The desire to develop self-control is birthed in self-respect. Self-control makes it possible to use other character qualities successfully. It helps children focus and finish things well.

The same is true for us. Being self-controlled means that situations may not have much power over us. We're more likely to maintain our excellent character. Our mood, the weather, and any other number of things won't change the way we relate to our children. Rather, our values, character, and purposes rule.

But exerting self-control requires energy. Baumeister and Tierney found that children asked to use self-control for too long without a break are more likely to struggle and give in to their yearnings.[4] I think it's true for adults, too. I know it's true for me. How many days did I do great on my food plan and then blow it at 10:00 pm? Far too many.

Children benefit from being allowed to take short, purposeful breaks while doing their chores and while studying. They'll need to be supervised at first so these breaks don't last thirty minutes long. They can learn to honor your system. Work fifteen, break for five. Creating shorter lessons and allowing children to do things like ten jumping jacks in between assignments is wise.

This type of modification is especially helpful for children diagnosed with ADHD and other similar challenges. We must compassionately understand that self-control can be difficult for them. This doesn't mean we don't talk about, teach it, or expect it. It does mean we make it easier for them to use self-control when we can.

"Chunk and Chew" might work well for you.[5] Your children spend 10 minutes concentrating on their reading, watching their assigned video, listening to you teach, and the like. Then they "chew" on what they learned for 2 minutes to process it. They could talk with you, write down a few things they remember, draw a picture relevant to the content, and more. This will help them be self-controlled longer in total and enhance their learning. It's a win-win.

The energy required to be self-controlled is another reason to prioritize resiliency. Resilient children who don't maintain their self-control for an entire assignment, chore, or day, won't let self-regret rule them. They'll bounce back.

> *A man without self-control is like a*
> *city broken into and left without walls.*
> —PROVERBS 25:28

Respect for others

Respecting others is high on my list because it can motivate children to use all other character qualities. For instance, when children respect others, they'll *want* to be honest, generous, attentive, flexible, and sincere. They listen with a heart to learn and believe. They want to trust. They want to do well. Therefore, they'll complain less when things are hard. They will argue less, listen more optimistically, and speak without issuing demands.

Another benefit of respect for others is that children will be more thoughtful and considerate. They may consider their siblings' schedules when choosing to practice the piano. They may offer to do a sister's chore because of a major assignment she needs to finish. They may finish their work early because they remember you're going out of town on a business trip. Now they have time to play a game with you. This choice to be flexible comes easier to resilient children.

Children will more easily respect parents, siblings, educators, and others who tell the truth, appropriately explain their decisions calmly rather than having a "because I said so" attitude, and freely admit mistakes. Then, they'll notice who apologizes and who asks for forgiveness when sin has ruled. When you're vulnerable and transparent, they respect you more. And they can now admit their failings. They won't have to hide their struggles when they realize you struggle, too.

Raising children to honor and esteem others, starting with you, can change the climate of your home. Respect, like the other qualities, affects much more than motivation. Because of technology's influence and authority failures your children are aware of, the title

> When I meet families at homeschool conventions and churches, I know if parents respect their children. It shows up.

of "parent" doesn't automatically guarantee respect. It might have in the "old days," but your attitudes, actions, and beliefs greatly influence whether children will respect you. Hypocrisy damages you and them. Inconsistency gets in the way. Favoritism doesn't help. Sometimes parents' behavior weakens children's motivation.

Of course, children benefit when their parents respect them and others. When I meet families at homeschool conventions and churches, I know if parents respect their children. It shows up. They introduce me to their children by name. Sometimes they tell me about one of their strengths or interests. If I ask a child a question, they let the child answer. They bend to make eye contact with them. They acknowledge them and engage with them.

> *Do nothing from selfish ambition or conceit, but in*
> *humility count others more significant than yourselves.*
> —PHILIPPIANS 2:3

Compassionate

Children who are compassionate feel people's pain and want to help them. As a result, they also don't want to inflict pain on others. This quality positively affects relationships and decision making. Compassion gives rise to acceptance, kindness, and gentleness. Compassion leads to service.

Compassionate children may be more aware than others that their parents are frustrated or overwhelmed. They don't want to add to their parents' pain so they will often obey them and do what's right. They may recognize we're frustrated with one child so they don't argue, but instead choose first-time obedience. Realistically, they might choose this decision because they want that brother to look worse in comparison. But often it's the good quality of compassion that drives these choices.

Do we choose to see our children's circumstances and respond appropriately? Although consistency is usually appropriate when raising and motivating children, if we don't have compassion and individualize our reactions and decisions when it's appropriate, why would our children? Modeling this character quality matters tremendously. How could our compassion show up? Do we give our daughter a break after a late night of babysitting? Do we joyfully do a son's chore for him after a tough loss on the field? Do we let our youngest son know his recent illness means our expectations for a test score are lower than normal?

Put on then, as God's chosen ones,
holy and beloved, compassionate hearts,
kindness, humility, meekness, and patience.
—COLOSSIANS 3:12

Brave

For children to make and act on right decisions requires them to be brave. For example, if they obey their parents in front of peers, they might get teased. If they study to do well on a test, their peers may ostracize them. If they try their best to sweep out the garage the way their dad explained the task, they risk having to do it again and again when their dad finds out they can do it. They also risk being told they did it wrong. All of this takes courage.

You need to be brave, too. I want you to parent strong and do what's right for your children even if they complain, push back, and say hateful things. I encourage you to parent so your children will be your friend when they're 25 rather than prioritizing friendship with them now. Parent with the long view in mind and bravely let them not like you now because of some of your choices.

> *Have I not commanded you? Be strong and courageous.*
> *Do not be frightened, and do not be dismayed,*
> *for the LORD your God is with you wherever you go.*
> —JOSHUA 1:9

Responsible

Children who are responsible (response-able) know what is expected of them and they do it. Like respecting others, this

CHARACTER: A SKILL AND A WILL   45

character quality can motivate children to use all the others. It leads to appropriate independence, including relying on themselves to motivate themselves and not always expecting others to provide the "carrot on the stick."

Did you notice my adjective "appropriate" in the above paragraph? That's there because of something my friend Lori Wildenberg wrote. I think it's related to the lack of responsibility parents tell me is near epidemic proportions in their homes. She got me thinking.

> I'm done falling for the independence lie. My goal isn't to raise independent children. My measure of success is to have responsible and caring kids who are able to rely on one another, ask for help and give help when needed, and trust the Lord throughout their lives. I don't want my young adults to become the Lone Ranger. I hope they will be more like the all for one and one for all Musketeers.[6]

What do you think? Do you see the relationship, too? If you allow your children to become too independent too soon, will they feel less necessary in the family unit? Will they be less inclined to step up, see something to do, and do it? Maybe. Lori writes that she wants to raise children who don't become Lone Rangers but the Three Musketeers instead.

Many parents I speak with tell me they're concerned about entitlement.

Also, the relationship among the character qualities here is relevant. If children aren't humble, they might believe others should serve them. If children don't respect themselves, they won't believe they can be responsible. Also, if they don't respect themselves, they don't care about their reputation. Therefore, they don't need to be responsible. If they don't have self-control, they'll be easily distracted and discouraged, which makes responsibility harder to bear. If they don't respect you, they don't want to follow your direction and accomplish what you ask them to do. Hello irresponsibility!

Many parents I speak with tell me they're concerned about entitlement. I am, too. Entitled kids don't want to be responsible for anything. With the I-deserve-it-all-now and it-better-be-easy mentality that's far too common, they want the easy way out. If this connection is relevant to you and your children, make time to talk about it.

Remember character is taught *and* caught. When you are responsible, you can motivate children to be. You'll disappoint them less and be more likely to apologize if you do. If you tell them you'll help with a project after dinner, you'll remember. You'll help them accomplish their goals, and you'll follow through with consequences, as necessary. They'll appreciate you and want to behave like this toward you and others.

Commit your work to the LORD,
and your plans will be established.
—PROVERBS 16:3

Initiative

When children take initiative, they recognize and do what needs to be done before being asked to do it. It's a beautiful companion to responsibility. This attribute of self-motivated children improves our relationships because we don't need to remind them of everything and nag them when they don't do what they're supposed to.

Children may never develop this quality if you remind them of everything they must do. Rather, it's birthed when you help them grow in appropriate independence. Would it surprise you to learn it's a key to thriving in the 21st century?[7]

Do you initiate action, or do you always wait for others? When you do what needs to be done when you see that it needs to be done, you accomplish more. There are fewer interpersonal conflicts, and peace reigns. Think about it—many tasks that help families and make a home run more smoothly aren't consistently assigned to a person. Someone needs to do them. When we step up, it's beautiful.

Whoever is slack in his work is a brother to him who destroys.
—PROVERBS 18:9

Effort, diligence, and perseverance

These three go hand in hand. Without effort, children can't be diligent. Without applying effort and choosing to be diligent, they won't be able to persevere. Talking with children about all three together is wise. Many children think effort is all that matters. They're wrong.

Effort is simply the *choice to work hard.* Effort sometimes requires physical power, sometimes mental power, and sometimes both. Diligence adds the idea of focus. It's *applying effort over time.* Perseverance is also something that happens over time, but adds the notion of being *persistent in spite of difficulties,* disappointments, discouragement, and the like. It's not just enough to work hard. Children give up (and sometimes parents do, too) because they forget that diligence and perseverance are often necessary choices for learning and obedience.

Did you notice the relationship there to resiliency? Good for you! Resilient children don't give up. Children who know the value of effort, diligence, and perseverance will have the character to try again.

Do your children sometimes talk so much about having a longer quiet time or doing their chores that they think they've done them? Do you ever talk so much about doing the dishes that you think you've done them? Have you been surprised to discover them dirty in the sink before heading to bed?

I tell children that "wishing it so won't make it so." You

could try Thomas Monson's "eight W" statement to get a reaction from your children: "Work will win when wishy washy wishing won't."[8]

I recognized this "wishing pattern" in my life often enough that I claimed Proverbs 14:23 as one of my life verses.

In all toil there is profit, but mere talk tends only to poverty.
—PROVERBS 14:23

When writing this book, I still needed to write my blog, film our weekly videos, post on social media, pay attention to the ministry's finances, meet with staff, prepare to speak, travel to events, and speak. I also went to church, had dinner with friends, worked out with my trainer, and took care of other responsibilities. Frustration grew as I wasn't staying focused when writing. I realized that diligence was the quality I was lacking—I wasn't applying effort over time. When I got bored, I jumped to a different task rather than staying focused on what I was doing. Usually, it wasn't that I needed to persevere. I wasn't always avoiding effort because something was difficult. I just didn't want to do it. I needed to be diligent. It helped me tremendously to figure out which quality I needed. Words matter. Definitions strengthen our understandings.

Scripture renews our mind and transforms our heart. Therefore, I chose to add Proverbs 21:5 and 12:24 to the above

Proverb to change my behavior. Memorizing them and talking about them with my accountability partners was very helpful.

The plans of the diligent lead surely to abundance,
but everyone who is hasty comes only to poverty.
—PROVERBS 21:5

The hand of the diligent will rule,
while the slothful will be put to forced labor.
—PROVERBS 12:24

Is it possible that your children may not be as motivated as you'd like because you rescue them too early, too often? I understand that you may not like seeing them "suffer" when they're persevering. However, if they don't learn to persevere in the safety of your home, they may never learn to. They'll always look for the easy way out. They'll quit jobs that demand too much time and end relationships that require too much effort. They won't care about the consequences. That's not what you want for them. I know you value the things you worked hard for. Don't rob children of that same satisfaction. Allow them to persevere.

Have you ever seen chicks about to hatch in an incubator? Maybe you noticed one egg moving a bit. That chick figured out it's not supposed to live in that cramped space forever. It begins to peck the shell. If you're watching these eggs in the incubator, you might conclude, *Oh! His time has come—he's about ready to come out of the egg! I'm going to rescue him!* And you gently crack open the eggshell and say, "Welcome to the world, little chick!" Do you know what will happen to that chick? It dies. It's the effort to peck its way out of the shell that develops its lungs and allows it to breathe and live.

> For a baby chick, it's the effort to peck its way out of the shell that develops its lungs and allows it to breathe and live.

"No effort equals death." Maybe you can post this sign where your children study. If that chick isn't willing to put forth effort, it dies in its shell. Also, if it decides, *Oh, that really hurts and it's hard work!* and it stops pecking, what happens? It dies. Your sign could also state, "No pain, no gain."

But, to be fair, you also should write on that same card, "Too much help equals death." Do you understand? If you rescue your child — "Welcome to the world, little chick!"—your son dies *potentially* because he never develops in the safety of your home, where he ought to be safe to try and to fail and to be loved unconditionally in the midst of that.

If this is your story, you are perfectly capable of having the hard conversation that might be necessary. Look your daughter in the eye and say, "You know what, Julia? We have made some mistakes. We have allowed your complaining to convince us to make chores and studying easier for you. But we were recently reminded that we're not doing you a favor at all. You need to learn to apply yourself, be diligent, and persevere through challenges. So, we're going to make some changes. At first, you may be confused. We're not mad at you. It's not about you; it's about us and our decisions. We need to return to values we say are important to us. Can you trust us to love you well and do what's best? Here's our first change . . ."

No matter the age of your children, I'm confident you're aware that you must apply effort as you raise your children. You must be diligent to stay focused on goals you have for them in this season. If you get distracted, so will they. Of course, perseverance is a quality effective parents share. Your children need you to not give up on yourself or them. When the going gets tough, keep going!

Pray for them, too. Prayer is a powerful tool—use it! Your personal and specific prayers for your children communicate your deep love for them and your dependence on God. Your prayers are a significant way your children learn who you hope they'll be and what you hope they'll do. Pray they'll develop a heart for Christ. Model and teach what they need for their heart to be transformed into His likeness. This will change their character and, therefore, their motivation and motives, too.

Character Qualities For Life

Do you know what's beautiful? Every one of these qualities that makes motivation easier for your children will serve them well in life. Prioritize them now to improve their motivation *and* to enhance their lives. Here are just a few ways these qualities matter:

Humility: Life will be fuller because this quality allows us to learn, grow, mature, and experience more.

Self-respect: This is an antidote to negativity and all forms of bullying. People who respect themselves can more easily react to negative influences and messages as if they're covered in Teflon. Nothing will stick.

Self-control: Having this quality makes it more likely we'll be productive. Our relationships will be healthier. We'll be less frustrated with ourselves and less likely to adopt negative behaviors and habits.

Respect for others: We'll develop rich relationships and look for opportunities to affect others positively. We'll serve and, therefore, develop strengths.

Compassion: We'll be fulfilled as we minister God's hope and healing to people in need. Our kindness and gentleness enhance relationships.

Bravery: When we're brave, we'll stand up for ourselves and others. We won't compromise our values. We'll advance what we believe in as we put ourselves out there. Aristotle said that "courage is the first of human qualities because it is the quality which guarantees the others."

Responsibility: Responsible adults own their junk and don't shift blame. They're honest, and they accomplish much. They're team players.

Initiative: Those who initiate action are not overly dependent on others. They're valued team members because they see what could be done and choose to do it.

Effort, diligence, and perseverance: Because of these qualities, we are productive. We don't give up on ourselves or others. We don't want to be defined by what we do, but this doesn't mean we shy away from doing what we can.

WHAT ABOUT YOU?

Do you understand more about how character affects motivation? The link between these two concepts is important. Can you think of a time in your life where lack of character to keep yourself motivated led to something you missed or didn't do because you weren't motivated to do it? Were there consequences? Do you have regrets about it? What did you do or have you done about it? When appropriate, share with your kids.

THINGS TO DO

- Do your children make excuses for everything? This decreases their confidence and weakens their resolve to be better and to do things better. And I know it can be very frustrating and cause arguments. Introducing them to the "Excuse Goose" might help.[9] Tell your children that the Excuse Goose looks for easy ways of doing things and always has an excuse for doing something wrong. It also has a habit of blaming others rather than taking responsibility. Discuss what the Excuse Goose should do instead. Make a commitment to not be like it. Do not let anyone in the family call someone an Excuse Goose in a mean way. If your children are mature enough, you could use the name to tell them when you hear them making excuses.

- As a fun way of evaluating your children's humility and self-respect, and probably other character qualities, too, have them lay down on a piece of butcher paper or buy paper tablecloths for this activity.[10] Draw around their body with a marker. You can lay on paper, too, and have them draw around you. (You could just make lists of the following, but some of your children will enjoy it more if you do the activity as described. Plus, because it's more creative, it may stimulate more accurate thoughts.)

  Now, on their head and shoulder areas, have them write what they're good at. (If your children are young, they can dictate their thoughts to you or an older sibling.) In the stomach area, have them write things they need to work on. On the arms, they write how they got good at things. On their legs, have them write what they can do to improve. (Change it up if you want; there's no significance of using the arms and legs.)

  How self-aware are they? Are you? Are strengths and challenges both appropriately included? Is it obvious that things they need to work on were easier to list? Are they not as aware of their strengths? Or are they aware of how they developed their skills and what they can do to improve? If not, change will be challenging, as we'll see in the next chapter.

- Also, you can compare their lists to what you listed in the activity at the end of chapter 1. Did you think of many more things than they did? What did they list that you didn't? Do you agree with them? Your children may enjoy critiquing what you list on your drawing. Of course, encourage respectful behavior as they interact with you and with siblings. As I wrote about earlier, they want to be known, understood, and loved. And, as you'll read about later, identity controls behavior. Who they think they are is who they will be. This activity has much power associated with it.

- If your children struggle with self-control, have them write out "if-then" statements for the relevant issues.[11] You can help them brainstorm or they can come up with their own ideas that you then react to. Their ownership of the ideas will be helpful. For example, "If I feel like I'm getting mad, I will . . ." Or, "If I feel like teasing Ricky when he makes mistakes, I will . . ."

- Read Appendix B from my friends Steve and Joyce Baker. They share how character can be taught as Jesus taught—with imitation, intentionally, individually, and with intensity. How do you think you're doing at each of these four? Set goals for yourself.

- Go to the book's website, www.StartWithTheHeart .net, and check out the suggestions for how to teach character qualities.

THINGS TO THINK ABOUT

- Spend some time choosing character qualities you want to prioritize in your family. Which of mine will you include? Consider your children's individual needs. Which other qualities will you include? What will you start with?

- Look the words up in a dictionary and use a thesaurus to broaden your understanding. Talk about the qualities with your children and see what they think the words mean. More importantly, how do they think someone behaves who has that quality? For example, what do they think initiative looks like for them? For you?

- Ask your children if they can make some commitments to prioritizing the qualities you choose. Ask how you can help them. What do you know you can do better to help them?

Sow a thought, and you reap an act.
Sow an act, and you reap a habit.
Sow a habit, and you reap a character.
Sow a character, and you reap a destiny.

UNKNOWN[11]

What Makes Change Happen?

Wow, chapter 2 sounded pretty great, right? But that was a lot of stuff! You may be asking, "How in the world can I get there when I struggle just to get my child to change his clothes?" Have you been there? Are you there now? I imagine every parent has been. Maybe your son loved his superhero PJs and wanted to wear them all day. Maybe your daughter put her favorite dress on for church, but it was too cold outside for her to wear it. Did one of your kids go through a sweatshirt phase?

As hard as it can be to get these kids out of one outfit and into another, getting them to change attitudes, actions, and beliefs can be more challenging. You know that—it's most likely among the reasons you bought this book. I'm grateful you care and haven't given up. Let me encourage you—you can learn how to help children change their attitudes, actions, thoughts, feelings, and beliefs, too.

You're interested in motivation because children need to make some changes. Right? Motivation and change are intertwined and inseparable. You'll also see how much work is sometimes necessary for motivation to work and to last. You will see what makes change happen.

Motivation, motive, and *move* all come from the same root. Motivation moves us. Motivation has been defined as "the force or energy that results in engagement."[1] The motive is key because it determines the direction of the movement and the type of engagement children choose. Some children are motivated to be "invisible" because it's less stressful, or they're just overwhelmed. Some are motivated to do every chore perfectly because it makes their brother look bad. Some don't want to do well at their piano lesson because they think they'll get assigned a difficult piece for their recital. Some children are motivated to be popular at any cost.

Can you see how these motives determine children's movement? These children will avoid some behaviors and embrace others. *For you to successfully motivate them toward different goals, you must first acknowledge the goals they prefer.* Now you will be able to help them stop, turn around, and move in a different direction.

From mediocrity to excellence.

Sadness to joy.

Fear to bravery.
Self-centeredness to others-centeredness.
Irresponsibility to responsibility.
Callousness to compassion.
From "I'm worthless" to "I matter."
"My parents don't understand me" to "I'll talk more with my parents."
"I can't" to "I'll try."
"It's too hard" to "I can ask for help."

Asking the Right Questions

This might surprise you, but all children are motivated. There's actually no such thing as a nonmotivated person. Children might *not* be motivated to learn, obey, and succeed and that's why you're frustrated. But these children *are* motivated—to remain apathetic, get into trouble, or fail.

It doesn't help to ask, "How do I get my kids motivated?" Rather, we need to ask, "How can I *redirect* their motivation?" For older kids, we might ask, "How can I present alternative goals so they'll want to move in a new direction?" Or, "What would it take for them to adjust their goals?" How about, "How do I help my children want what is good for them? What would it take for them to be motivated for the things I want them to value? How can I guide and redirect their desire and motivation?"

For example, are any of these scenarios familiar?

Child's goal: Get a "B" on the test to keep pressure at bay.

Child thinks: *A "B" is good enough, and I know I can get that. I don't want the pressure of trying for and getting an "A" because everyone will decide I can keep getting them. Then what if I can't?*
You wonder: *Why doesn't Alixa ever get an "A"? Why is she satisfied with "Bs" all the time? She knows her education matters.*

Child's goal: Get out of cleaning my bathroom in the future.

Child thinks: *I don't like cleaning my bathroom. It's boring, and I don't care how dirty it gets. It's mine. Maybe Mom will get so frustrated with the poor job I do that she'll just do it instead of making me do it.*
You wonder: *What's it going to take for Joshua to take care of his bathroom? I'm sick of getting on him all the time.*

Child's goal: Prove I'm better than James by getting a higher score on this game today.

Child thinks: *I'm so close to James's score. I know I'm better than he is, so I'm not quitting until I get a higher score.* You wonder: *Why is that game so important to him? There are more important things he should be doing! How do I get him to see that?*

It would sure help if children had an internal GPS to warn them when they should change goals and directions. Not too long ago, while driving a rental car and trying to find my hotel, I appreciated the "redirect" announcement after I turned too soon. Imagine if our kids came with this internal voice!

Some kids *need* to change direction. Until they figure that out, you need to be their GPS telling them to make a U-turn or make other small adjustments.

Where Change Starts:
Erasing Lies, Embracing Truths

The most important conclusion for me to pass on to you relevant to helping children change is that beliefs cause behavior. There are reasons we do what we do. Without wrestling with beliefs and working to see if lies are embedded in them, permanent change is unlikely. We must erase lies and embrace truths.

Have you been trying to motivate your daughter to be respectful? Does she roll her eyes, impatiently listen, talk back, and argue? I can get her to stop rolling her eyes at you so you'll see them. I can teach her to appear to listen and to be silent rather than question everything you say. But none of these changes means she respects you.

Read that paragraph again. Do you understand? Changing outward behavior or even eliminating it entirely doesn't necessarily mean your daughter now respects you. You may assume she does and then be angrier than before when discovering based on her behavior that she doesn't. She has simply faked it to make it.

When wanting to find solutions, your question must be, "Why is my daughter disrespecting me?" and not "Why is my child rolling her eyes?" Do you see the difference? One question is about the cause. One is about the symptom or evidence.

I was privileged to talk with 13-year-old twin boys who were disrespecting their dad. They knew it and they wanted to stop, but their negative behaviors continued. They didn't ask him for help when trying to solve problems, they questioned his ideas, and generally looked down on him.

Guess what the cause was? During our discussion, one of the boys figured it out. He excitedly declared, "Our dad doesn't have any brothers or sisters. He can't understand what it's like to share everything with my brother. Sometimes sharing and never having privacy is really hard!" This discovery didn't immediately eliminate the disrespect, but it gave the boys and their dad and mom something practical to talk about. Their parents made it clear that knowing a reason was helpful, but no reason makes disrespect okay. This is very important: reasons are not excuses.

The dad learned to ask more questions about the boys' feelings and attitudes. The boys appreciated his desire to understand their situation better. The mom, who did have siblings, shared some of her experiences growing up with them to further help her husband relate to their sons.

Put Off, Put On

Because of my frustrations when trying to change some behaviors many years ago, I turned to two of many trustworthy sources for me—Scripture and the dictionary. Scripture is certainly much more important. Yet the dictionary is often insightful and beneficial. There I discovered change can actually mean "to *ex*change." That was a huge "aha" moment for me and totally lined up with one of my go-to Bible passages about change: Ephesians 4:22–24.

Changing anything is like changing around from one outfit to another. I need to know what to take off *and* what to put on. And so do you and your children. If you just try to take off the old, negative behavior, without thinking about what to replace it with, the change probably won't last long. You have to wear something. If you don't replace the negative with something better, the past behavior may return or something worse may take its place.

Just making statements like these can be empowering:

- I need to take off arguing and put on first-time obedience.
- I need to take off bullying and put on kindness.
- I need to take off distractions and put on focus.
- I need to take off "I don't want to" and put on "Do it anyway."

Scripture consistently provides the biggest of all "aha" experiences for me. I hope you can say the same. God's Word is true, rich, relevant, and practical. It is life. Reading for truths about change provided great fruit. Look what I read in Ephesians 4:22–24:

Put off your old self, which
belongs to your former manner of life
and is corrupt through deceitful desires,
and to be renewed in the spirit of your minds,
and to put on the new self, created after the likeness
of God in true righteousness and holiness.

WHAT MAKES CHANGE HAPPEN? 69

I see three biblical components to change. Do you see them?

1. **Take off your old self.** The first application of this idea is to our salvation. We take off our old unbelieving, doubting self. Then we can also apply this to our unacceptable and sinful attitude, behavior, thought, feeling, or belief. Note! Not everything you don't like about yourself or your children should be taken off. It's not all "old." God may want you to be "quirky." Maybe you're supposed to be a "Chatty Kathy" like me. Your son's sensitivity might be his greatest strength. Your daughter's analytical nature was chosen for her by God. So was her petite stature. Her attitude toward it may need to change, though.

   This first step in the change process is to identify what to take off—what attitude, behavior, thought, feeling, or belief is unhealthy and possibly sinful that I no longer want to "wear" anymore? What do I *need* to take off even if I don't want to?

2. **Renew the spirit of your mind; "make it new."** Renewing the mind comes by the work of the Holy Spirit and our pursuing the promptings He gives us to get

to know God's love, mind, presence, and grace. This happens through prayer, by reading the Bible, listening to Truth, worshiping, and being in close and meaningful relationships with other Christians. When renewing your mind, God will show you what beliefs are causing the attitude, behavior, thought, or feeling you've decided to take off in step 1. These beliefs must be replaced with truths for change to last. For example, time with God might help your daughter realize she is angry at Him for making her short. She may also see that she's feeling inferior because of her lack of height. Changing these beliefs can result in changes to attitudes, behaviors, thoughts, or feelings.

Interviews with kids have taught me how pervasive beliefs like these can be. You think these beliefs are just relevant to your daughter's height. They're not. Because she's angry at God, perhaps she has lost hope and stopped praying. Her feelings of inferiority can negatively affect her friendships and even her studying. *Nothing about me matters.*

This "make it new" process often reveals additional things to take off that you didn't know about when making the list in step 1. Pay attention and be open to new insights. Sometimes taking off two or three things at the same time is very effective because they're related and rooted in the same lies.

3. **Put on the new self.** These are the Christlike and God-honoring attitudes, behaviors, thoughts, feelings, and beliefs that help you behave more like God. For instance, in general, Scripture suggests we can and should put on love, joy, peace, patience, kindness, goodness, faithfulness, gentleness, and self-control (Galatians 5:22–23). The Beatitudes, recorded for us in Matthew 5:2–12, also provide relevant general ideas about what to "wear." Here we learn that God wants us to be desperately dependent upon Him, to mourn, and to hunger and thirst for righteousness. He wants us to be meek, merciful, pure in heart, peacemakers, and behave in such a way that we might be persecuted for righteousness' sake.

Because Ephesians 4:24 teaches us to "put on the new self," which starts with God, you'll also want to read and study the Bible for specifics. Did God do anything or say anything directly related to what you want to take off or what you want to put on? Your daughter might discover she was "fearfully and wonderfully made" (Psalm 139:14) and created in the image of God (Genesis 1:27). She may then conclude she is not inferior. Discovering that God looks at our hearts may help her put her height in proper perspective (1 Samuel 16:7).

Your daughter can now take off her negative attitude toward her height, her anger toward God, and her feelings of inferiority. She can replace these with contentment about her height and a belief God did a good thing when He made her the way He did. With further study, she can discover more.

Colossians 3:1–17 is the other passage the Spirit directed me to. Here, we're instructed to "put to death" whatever is earthly, and "put on the new self, which is being renewed in knowledge after the image of its creator." You might want to check out the list of specific "clothes" to put on.[2] The fourteenth verse is significant: "And above all these put on love, which binds everything together in perfect harmony."

Things to Think About
as You're Working on Changing

So, based on these guidelines, there *are* effective ways you can help your child—and, more important, yourself—bring about desired change. Let me share several profitable insights I've discovered about this change process. They will help you use it in your life and then with your children. I do encourage you to use this for an issue in your life before you think it through with a child's issue in mind. You'll have more confidence helping children use it if you have personally experienced its benefits.

Because of God's grace...

Throughout the use of the change process, remember God's grace is available for all—His unmerited favor. He chooses to bless us because we are His. Grace isn't earned through obedience. It is God's gift to you. Talk about it, and display grace toward yourself and your children because they are your children. We are free when we understand that we do not *need* to change because God is angry or He won't love us in our messy situation and sin.

Decide for yourself why you want to change. Is it because Christ's love compels you? (2 Corinthians 5:14). This change process has become a lifeline for me—truly. It works. I hope you'll successfully use it often.

Relying on God, we won't burn out. We will work from an inward motivation of God's love for us and our love for Him. Love is compelling!

It's never just one thing

Discovering that many negative issues are connected has been a very revealing benefit of using this strategy. I've been disappointed to discover there wasn't one issue I was struggling with but several. Using this process helped me understand why change was taking longer than I thought it should. I had only dealt with one issue, not recognizing the web of sin entangling me. There may be more than one attitude, action, or belief involved.

> **I've been disappointed to discover that there wasn't one issue I was struggling with but several.**

For instance, working on interrupting revealed how impatient and self-centered I was, especially in certain circumstances. Irresponsibility can be connected to fear, being overwhelmed, and a lack of knowledge about how to do something. Laziness can be connected to perfectionism, fatigue, and a lack of purpose.

When choosing an issue to "take off," grab a pen and paper and make a list. Reflect on when and where the negative issue you want to take off commonly shows up. Think about the triggers. Ask the Spirit to show you connections to other negatives. This can be overwhelming and freeing at the same time. You may discover for the first time why you haven't been very successful overcoming an issue.

Brainstorm many things to "wear"

The longer the list of things you can "wear" instead of what you've been "wearing," the greater the likelihood you'll change. Brainstorming will allow you to get out of your box and think creatively. What are the opposites of what you want to take off?

For instance, you may recognize you have fallen into a habit of complaining so you decide to work on it before you direct your children to work on the same problem. You could "wear" contentment, compassion, hope, joy, satisfaction, peace, and silence.

Maybe you struggle with procrastination. You could "wear" getting organized, asking for help, being willing to make mistakes, responsibility, setting small goals, being obedient, and using positive self-talk.

I've found that trusting a friend can help in this process. If you've behaved in the troublesome way you'd like to change for a while, opposite, healthy behaviors might not be obvious to you. Or you might not have enough hope that you can behave in those better ways to even list them. Asking a friend who doesn't struggle in the same area may help. Better yet, find someone who used to struggle, but has overcome the problem.

Searching Scripture can identify new attitudes and actions,

too. Often when there's a Scripture about the negative you want to take off, there's either a positive mentioned or implied. This is especially true in Proverbs where, for example, fools and wise ones are contrasted" (see Proverbs 12:15, 26:12). Look for this hope.

Behaviors, beliefs, circumstances

Remember the key truth I presented earlier: beliefs *cause* behavior. It's also valuable to recognize that some behaviors influence other behaviors. Have you noticed that sometimes making healthier choices in one area of your life automatically improves other behaviors? For instance, fatigue is often mentioned when I ask parents why children struggle with different character qualities. So it's possible that some of children's attitudes, thoughts, feelings, and behaviors will improve when they simply get more sleep.

Humbly, we need to recognize that our behaviors often influence our children's behaviors. For example, if we ignore them and they feel invisible, they may disrespect us. If we aren't grateful, our children may act entitled, too. If we play favorites, children are affected.

It's important to understand that each of these behaviors we choose is rooted in beliefs. So although changing behaviors will influence other behavior, to permanently make better choices, the foundational beliefs for each contributing behavior need to be identified and changed. Now we're back to the power of beliefs.

For example, are you ignoring your children because you believe you need to keep your online friends happy by liking their posts and commenting on them? Are you ungrateful because you've been comparing yourself to others? Are you playing favorites because you're angry at a child who disappointed you? Do you believe he was old enough to know better?

Our circumstances are also influential. Have you just moved into a new home? You and the kids will have many distractions, and it's been harder to maintain

Identifying beliefs causing negative behaviors is essential.

consistency. Did someone important to a child pass away or move away? Did your child not make the basketball team or cheerleading squad?

We should understand the role of circumstances and be compassionate toward ourselves and our children. At the same time, we should not give our circumstances any more power than is appropriate. What's out of our control shouldn't control us long.

Causes are not excuses

A sign of maturity is not letting causes become excuses for

your behavior. If you humble yourself and allow the Spirit to reveal causes to you, you may see all kinds of things on the list.

Perhaps the way you were parented is a reason. It's not an excuse. Perhaps your personality causes you to clash more often with one child than another. That's not an excuse. Your strengths might contribute to issues that cause problems. For example, my strength as an exhorter can cause me to interrupt and teach when people just wanted to be heard. Strengths are not an excuse.

Being humble and compassionate toward yourself and others is a must. However you have responded in the past is okay. You didn't know this then. You do now, and I hope you're more hopeful than discouraged—full of courage and ready to give it a try.

Kill the spiders!

As I explained, identifying beliefs causing negative behaviors and unhealthy attitudes is essential. If you don't identify them and replace them with positive truths, I can almost guarantee that the negatives will return. Or you'll battle in your own strength to keep them at bay. That can be exhausting and steal your joy.

If you clean your house and sweep away every spider web, you feel great, right? You should. But what often happens? Spider webs come back. Why? Because you didn't find and kill the spider. That's the same principle here. Find the causes (there's rarely only one) of the issue and kill them. Then replace them with truth to result in more permanent change.

Let's revisit the issue of complaining. It's true that you'll benefit from more contentment, compassion, hope, joy, satisfaction, peace, and silence. But just "wearing" those over complaining won't work. When old triggers occur, complaining will likely begin again. Then you'll be frustrated, become discouraged, give up . . . Sound familiar? I can relate! Don't beat yourself up.

Many, many people, of all ages, struggle with this. Admitting it happens to you should increase your compassion for children. They don't have your maturity or experiences, so identifying beliefs that cause behaviors—and killing them— isn't easy for them.

What could be causing the complaining? Perhaps you believe, "I have a right to what I want when I want it." (Spider!) Maybe you are judging your life based on others, and you no longer feel good about things. (Spider!) Maybe your dreams haven't come true. (Spider!)

Be willing to get quiet somewhere and search your heart. Possibly ask a spouse or trusted friend to help you see what's changed and what the root issues of your behaviors might be. What beliefs might be driving your behavior that you need to "kill"? Are there contributing behaviors you need to change? Definitely pray.

Replace Lies with Truth

Thinking of and listing reasons for your negative behaviors is revealing. I can almost guarantee that you'll find healthy and understandable reasons for your behaviors. These need to be understood and adjusted, not necessarily eliminated.[3]

"Disrespect" is a huge issue for parents and kids. Let's look at some of the causes my Facebook community listed for disrespect. Poor modeling from parents and on the TV shows they allow kids to watch and in songs they allow them to listen to were the most common causes, mentioned by 27% of the responders. These are choices and behaviors parents can change. Clearly, the parents' behaviors and the shows and songs are creating beliefs causing kids' behaviors.

The second most popular response was fatigue. Mentioned by 17%, this is something parents can change by respecting their children's bedtime and adjusting the number of activities their kids participate in. Also, when realizing a child's disrespect is caused by fatigue, we can have compassion and not be as disappointed in their behaviors. We don't excuse their disrespect necessarily, but we also don't label them as disrespectful children. When we change this behavior—a lack of sleep —we should see a change in their behavior. If not, then we'll want to look for other causes.

A child's sense of *being* disrespected was also mentioned by 17% of my Facebook friends. Is this relevant for you? Do you think you disrespect your children? Do others? In this reality, you may need to make some changes to your behavior. Children also need to change their belief from *when I'm disrespected, I can disrespect them* to *how I'm treated should not change how I treat others.* Might there be other beliefs involved? Maybe *because they hurt me, I have a right to hurt them.*

"Being frustrated by parents" was mentioned by 15% of those who responded. They specifically listed unclear communication and unfair expectations. Again, if this is relevant for you, you're the first one who needs to change behavior *and* beliefs. What's causing your communication to be unclear? What needs to change so your expectations are fair and communicated so your children believe they can be who you want them to be and do what you want them to do?

When identifying spiders that must be killed for new behaviors to last, renewing your mind with the Word of God is significant. It's too easy to say you can replace interrupting with waiting your turn, hate with love, irresponsibility with responsibility, and rudeness with kindness.

Remember that the 24th verse of Ephesians 4 teaches us to "put on the new self, created after the likeness of God." Therefore, searching Scripture for concepts related to the lies you need to replace with truth is relevant. These very purposeful studies will encourage you. God also speaks to us through messages from pastors, teachings we hear online, conversations with friends, worship, and books.

Is there anything relevant you can learn from God's behavior? Jesus' behavior? The Holy Spirit? Did He say anything specifically about your lies? You can also search to see if James, Timothy, Paul, and others wrote something relevant. What Proverbs are relevant? And which of the many one-another passages in the New Testament speaks to this issue (e.g., honor one another, be gentle with one another, carry one another's burdens)?

Meditating on the Scriptures the Holy Spirit draws me to has always been helpful. You can write them out, study them with cross-references, memorize them, and turn them into prayers. There's no answer key for this. It's a personal study between you and God. Change most likely won't be instantaneous, but it will be more lasting than if you didn't do this. Plus, time in the Word is never wasted.

What you discover will motivate you to rethink the lies, believe truth, and now choose to "wear" those. As the new beliefs drive new behaviors, you'll become even more sure of the truths. You'll often discover additional beliefs to rely on.

Change is a process, not an event. You may need to take off and replace behaviors and beliefs for the foreseeable future. Habits rarely change overnight. Permanent changes are possible because God is good. But especially if you're dealing with long-standing issues or the behavior is related to several others, the behavior may crop up occasionally. Don't give up and don't let your kids give up.

Why Change Can Be Challenging

All change is hard at first, messy in the
middle and so gorgeous at the end.
Robin Sharma[4]

Even when implementing the change process well, there may be times it doesn't appear to be working. If you can identify why your children are resistant to change, you'll be able to make changes and then motivate them to change effectively.

As I explained in chapter 1, if your relationship isn't healthy, your children may not care what you think. Starting with the heart matters! Also, if they're not resilient, they'll stay down after being disappointed and may not want to risk trying to change again. Failure is too painful.

Sometimes *we're* not helpful, "yelling and telling" instead of teaching. Maybe we're not modeling what we expect from them and our children are legitimately confused, disappointed, and angry. Sometimes they're overwhelmed.

But there are other things that get in the way of meaningful change . . .

Technology makes many things easy

I'm grateful that technology has made many things easier. For example, not only can we use a device to check into flights before we get to the airport, but I just checked into a hotel room and synced my phone to their system so it will open my hotel room door. No more worries about handling my luggage, briefcase, and purse while getting out my room card as I arrive at my door.

A potential problem exists when children want everything to be easy—even nontechnological things. Of course, not everything has a quick-fix, and they won't be happy all the time. But to try to stay happy they may resist change in general and the hard work it sometimes requires. I said it this way in my book, *Screens and Teens: Connecting with Our Kids in a Wireless World*:

> Teens tend to avoid things they can't do well in order to stay happy. Correcting mistakes, persevering, and asking for help makes them uncomfortable and insecure. They want things to be easy, and they cut-and-run or x-out when they're not. They're used to the identity of "I can do it myself."[5]

If your children are resilient and if you prioritize character qualities like initiative, effort, diligence, and perseverance, they will improve and grow in a world where many of their peers won't. Stay strong and parent long. You can do this!

Neurons that fire together, wire together

Habits are harder to break than attitudes and behaviors that haven't become entrenched. As I explain in the same book, "Patterns in the brain form because of repetition, much like water forces a pattern into the dirt when the river is first formed. When the same things (good or bad) are done over time, it's easy for us to keep doing them. Just like the water can't control where it goes. . . . A pattern has been set that can be hard to change. It becomes routine, a new normal."[6]

Do your kids complain a lot? Complaining makes more complaining easy. Are they irresponsible? Being irresponsible will be their default. Are they satisfied with a B or C when you know they're capable of earning an A? Not pushing themselves becomes their norm.

When you recognize your kids aren't changing successfully because the things that frustrate you have become habits, compassion is a great first response. Habits are hard to break! Let's be honest about this. You'll also need to be consistent and humble. Why humble? Because the chances are very good that you either exhibit the same habit or have contributed to your kids' development of it.

A carrot on a stick is all that works

Are your children motivated to change only when you're there with the offer of a reward when they're good and a punishment when they're not? Kids who depend on you, or others, to offer a good enough carrot on a stick will struggle to change on their own.

For example, you might say things like, "If you're dressed and ready by the time I come to your room to check on you, I'll get you a snack for the car ride." Or, "If you don't put your phone down right now, I'll take it away for the rest of the day!" You are trying to motivate them to make wise choices with external pressure. This extrinsic motivation can work, but should never be what we depend upon.

People aren't the only source of extrinsic (external) motivation. Things provide extrinsic motivation, too. For instance, a higher score on a game, earning a lead in the play if they rehearse more, the threat of a bad grade, and money offered when they do their chores well without complaining are all examples of extrinsic motivation.

WHAT ABOUT YOU?

As you've explored this "change process," what did you learn about yourself and how God reveals truth to you? Were you surprised by beliefs driving your behavior or how many behaviors are connected, therefore making change more challenging? What else makes change challenging? How will you overcome this and be an example of change to your children?

THINGS TO DO

- Pick one issue in your life and utilize this change process. This will increase your confidence when helping a child work through the process so their motivation improves. Choose an attitude or behavior you'd like to stop. You might want to start by asking yourself why you've been resistant to change or unsuccessful. If you're not sure, you could ask someone who knows you well. Sometimes we can't figure it out on our own.

- As you gain confidence in this process, choose one motivational dilemma for one child and apply the process. As you continue to think in these terms, the process will become more and more natural.

THINGS TO THINK ABOUT

- What have you successfully changed? How and why were you successful? Celebrate your success.

- What has one of your children successfully changed? How and why was he or she successful? Can any of those things be used for another issue? How can you celebrate your child's success?

- What are the most relevant reasons change isn't happening for you and/or your children? Why? And what can you do about it?
- How does praying for your children affect you and them?

Holy Spirit, I cannot know God better apart from your work. So my prayer is simple: keep me hungry for the knowledge of God. Don't let lesser breads satisfy this craving. Don't let lesser waters slake this thirst. Keep revealing more and more of Jesus to me. Humble me with his glory. Astonish me with his beauty. Mesmerize me with his mercy. Buckle my knees with his affections. Change me by his grace. Free me for his purposes. For indeed, "the people who know their God shall stand firm and take action" (Dan. 11:32). I pray in Jesus' all-consuming name. Amen.

SCOTTY SMITH[7]

The Five Core Needs

If you've done your very best to help children change, but they boomerang back to their old selves quickly, there might be something else you need to understand—your children's basic needs. I have identified what I call "the five core needs," and in this chapter we will look at them in depth.

How do these needs relate to that "boomerang" effect? It's possible that the positive behavior or attitude your children began to exhibit didn't have a firm foundation to support it. Secondly, in a warped way, maybe a negative attitude or behavior is meeting several or all five of their needs. Or several negatives might be involved. I share examples of this in these pages to help you understand.

Your children will need new, healthy ways to meet their needs so they can stop depending on the old attitudes and actions. Did you see the change process there? Taking off unhealthy ways of meeting needs and replacing them with authentic ways might be the most important change to make.

Tedd Tripp encourages us with these thoughts:

Children rarely run from a home where their needs are met. Who would want to walk out on a relationship in which he feels loved and respected? What child would run from someone who understands him, understands God and His ways, understands the world and how it works and is committed to helping him be successful?[1]

But first, let's look at those core needs . . .

Five Core Needs

God created you and your children with five core, basic needs that must be met.[2] These needs are interrelated. The health of one influences the others. Security is the foundation, followed by identity, belonging, purpose, and competence. Ponder these definitions. In what ways are your needs being met? What about your children?

Security—Who can I trust? People need security to be emotionally and physically safe and free from danger, fear, and anxiety. Security is healthiest when people trust God for their salvation and rely on Him and trustworthy, dependable, and honest people.

Identity—Who am I? People need identity to know who they are. Identity is healthiest when people know they are

THE FIVE CORE NEEDS   91

intentionally and uniquely designed by God and value this and their other identities so they have a current, honest, and complete view of who they are.

Belonging—Who wants me? People need belonging to be accepted and to connect with ease to others. Healthy belonging results from a growing relationship with God and strong relationships with trustworthy people.

Purpose—Why am I alive? People need purpose to know why they are alive. Purpose is healthiest when people have hope and discover and use their God-given passions to glorify Him and positively influence the world.

Competence—What do I do well? People need competence to do well with what they were created to do. Competence is healthiest when people rely on God, character, and decision making and work at developing their God-given abilities.

As you can see, children (and adults) are healthiest when we meet these needs in dependable, consistent, and authentic ways. They'll have a solid foundation for life. God's ways are best. He meets our needs and provides answers to these core questions in His holy Word.

Because the needs must be met, if healthy ways seem out of reach or actually are out of reach, children (and adults) will meet their needs in unhealthy or unwise ways. When this happens, the way they're trying to meet their needs must change in order for their behaviors to change. Are these examples relevant to you?

Security: Children may put their security in some *thing* rather than in trustworthy people. This will be troublesome because things don't last. For example, your daughter may feel secure when she believes she's the most beautiful one in the room. When someone cuter arrives, she has a bad hair day, or you ask her to wear something she doesn't think she looks good in, she may react badly. Her unhealthy view of security may be the cause of the arguments about clothes you're trying to decrease. It may explain your daughter's obsession with her appearance and how others look that day. To motivate her to change her goals and these behaviors, you need to help her place her legitimate need for security in people who have demonstrated qualities like dependability, honesty, and kindness. If she doesn't, she won't be motivated to give up the way she's trying to meet her need for security.

Identity: Children who only have a negative identity will have a hard time changing the behaviors it's based on. They need to know more about themselves to have the confidence to change. Do your children only know they never get anything done? Do you tell them often that they're lazy and they never do what they're told? To motivate these children to get their work done in a timely manner, you'll need to talk with them about their other identities. Eventually they can change from slow to quick, from incomplete workers to complete, and from lazy to diligent, but only if they have other answers to the "Who am I?" question.

Belonging: Children may try to meet their need for belonging by being popular. Therefore, they have to behave in ways that keep them popular. This might include being a class clown, being the gossip who knows what's going on with others, and underperforming to gain acceptance by peers who matter to them. To motivate them to change these behaviors, you need to help children devalue this type of popularity and discover healthier ways to meet their legitimate need for belonging.

Purpose: If children think their purpose is to be in control, they'll need to be in charge of their siblings and boss others, as well. They won't take direction well, if at all. If these are the behaviors you're trying to motivate them to change, you'll need to help them choose a different purpose. Then they'll be able to stop bossing others.

Competence: Children often confuse or equate competence, doing things well, with perfection, doing things without error. When this happens, even a slight error can discourage children so they don't want to try again. Or another common problem with competence can be children who base it on how others do. They may only feel competent when they're the best. Now, when a sibling or member of their peer group consistently does better, their competence evaporates. They're crushed. To motivate them to try again, you'll need to redefine competence.

How the Five Needs Are Connected

Changing behaviors without paying attention to all five core needs is almost impossible. They're related. If you don't take the time to see how each need might be informing children's choices, attitudes, and actions, at best, changes will be short-lived.

> Changing behaviors without paying attention to all five core needs is almost impossible.

The five needs build on one another—and there is a hierarchy, leading to *the* most important need. Let me explain.

Competence: What do I do well?

Many children and adults believe that perfection should be the goal. This is often related to technology. The operating systems are remarkable, and they seemingly don't do anything wrong. Facebook photo albums and videos posted by moms also suggest perfection is the goal.

They may believe perfection is what you expect because you correct every error and point out every false statement. You may become quickly frustrated and then angry when they make mistakes. You might also be modeling that you don't accept your own mistakes when things don't go perfectly well for you. (In later chapters, I'll address healthy ways to point out children's mistakes and how to talk about your frustration so they don't develop a perfectionistic attitude toward themselves.)

If perfection is their goal, they may avoid situations they think will be hard. They won't eagerly approach learning something new. They may panic at mistakes, not ask for help and hide from you when they don't know something, and quit trying because the risk of not measuring up is too great.

Developing the competence they need or want will be very hard for them. You and your children weren't created by God to be perfect. None of us were. I tell children that perfection is the destination—heaven with the One who is perfect—but excellence and competence are the journey.

Talk with your children about competence and its connections to the other core needs.

Purpose: Why am I alive?

God created all of us on purpose with purpose. Some purposes are relevant to everyone—to become who God intended us to be when He chose to create us, to glorify God, to worship God, to evangelize, to learn, and more. Other purposes are specific to us.

When children have ideas about what their specific purposes are and how they can fulfill the general ones, they will be much more motivated to develop the competencies they need. It works in reverse, too. When children believe they are competent, because they've worked hard and you affirmed their strengths, they may believe there are reasons to be alive. When they're not sure what those reasons might be, their strengths can point them in a specific direction.

If children don't believe they were created on purpose with purpose to fulfill, they won't be as interested in improving skills or achieving mastery.[3] Without purpose and a vision for their tomorrows, they think they don't need to be good at anything. In addition to helping them work on their competence by teaching them to improve their weaknesses and further develop their strengths, talk about their purposes. Reasons they're alive can provide the motivation they need to take risks and persevere when things are challenging.

I still remember when I realized that practicing to play a viola solo in church was an act of worship. I was 12 and religious at the time. As the music and lyrics of *How Great Thou Art* became real to me, I interpreted my opportunity differently. This was not going to be like playing at school or for my grandparents with my brother and cousins.

It wasn't until I was on the church platform playing the song that I was certain the lyrics on my sheet of music were true. My playing was now about God, not the people in the pews. I don't ever want to forget this shift and how I felt.

Looking back, I know my reasons motivated me to learn to play beautiful pieces of music throughout college. My purpose, glorifying and worshipping God, drove my desire for competence.

Music was also a way my brother, Dave, and I connected. We grew up with music as a priority, but it wasn't until college that we played together. We played in band together one year as undergraduates at Purdue University and in wind ensemble during graduate school. It's no surprise to those who know us and Dave's wife, Debbie, that many of our Christmas traditions involve music.

Purpose can connect people and, therefore, strengthen belonging. Belonging can help children discover and then believe in their purpose. This is a reason the quality of your relationship with your children matters to motivation. The better you know them and the more consistently you love them, the more they'll believe you when you tell them they need to do something better. You'll have reasons and they'll be willing to listen to them.

Observe to see how purpose is relevant to your children's challenges. Talk about this.

Belonging: Who wants me?

There are other ways purpose and belonging connect. Children who know their purpose will often choose to look for peers with similar goals and interests. They will want to hang out with people who affirm them and their purpose and be willing to end relationships that are not joyful and purposeful. These decisions strengthen belonging.

Being wanted is powerful. When children know they're wanted, it's more likely they'll believe they were created on purpose with something valuable to contribute. When their relationships are healthy and they listen to people who are on their side, they'll have greater stability and confidence. Their friends are likely to affirm them, point out their strengths, and talk optimistically about the future. This allows them to dream more about their reasons to be alive and pursue different competencies. Do you see how the core needs of belonging, purpose, and competence are interrelated?

Serving others, one of our main purposes, is directly influenced by belonging. Having healthy relationships makes this easier. Groups of friends may work together on service

projects. Serving together is also a significant advantage of joining and getting
involved at a church. Many have ongoing and seasonal opportunities to connect with like-minded people to make
a difference for others. As I write about

**Being wanted
is powerful.**

in *Screens and Teens*, serving together as a family is extra rich
because of the conversations you can have with your children
about how the experiences affect you and them.[4]

Children can serve alone, but it can be harder for them to
maintain their service. This won't be true if they're allowed to
serve with their strengths and interests (identity) and in ways
they can fulfill identified purposes. For example, if your son
is a soccer player, encourage him to start kicking a soccer ball
near where you're distributing Christmas gifts to the needy.
Children will soon play with him, and he'll feel confident because he was effective. Now he may want to volunteer again.

Serving motivates children to develop character and skills
because they are necessary. Serving builds overall confidence,
decreases self-centeredness, develops compassion for others,
and can lay a lifetime foundation where giving to others is second nature. Becoming others-centered through acts of service
is a process for many children. Do you see how this is related
to healthy belonging?

Belonging also directly influences *competence*.[5] Children who feel disconnected will more likely give up.[6] If you believe your children aren't motivated to improve their attitudes, skills, and behaviors, could it be that they have negative people influencing them? Do these people not value your children's competencies? Do they communicate these beliefs to your children?

What about your relationship with your children? Is your "belonging" healthy? If you talk more about what they can't do than what they can do, they may doubt their competence. Because of this negative orientation, you won't have much credibility to encourage them. Now, without confidence in their competence, they may doubt they have purpose.

So much of parenting requires walking a fine line. You do need to point out the things that challenge your children. Otherwise they won't know how they might hurt others and they won't know what to work on. But you also need to know and talk about their strengths. This will strengthen your belonging and increase your influence over your children. (Chapter 9 is full of wisdom about how to compliment and correct well. You'll love it!)

Talk with your children about how belonging is relevant to their challenges.

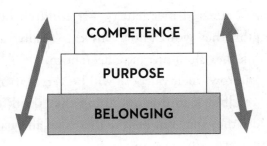

Identity: Who am I?

Just like children rarely if ever ask the other core needs questions out loud, don't expect your children to come to you and ask, "Who am I?" Yet, answers to this question not only form their identity, they are a key to the authentic and complete development of belonging, purpose, and competence.

Belonging is affected by identity—If children only know what's wrong about themselves, they'll doubt anyone will want them. Or they may only connect with peers with similar weaknesses. This may mean they don't want to change because they can't risk losing their friends. Their need for belonging must be met.

When children's identity is positive, they're likely to have more healthy relationships. Think back to when you were young. How did what you knew about yourself influence your belonging? For me, several things stand out. Dance in the elementary years. Orchestra and band in my teen years. An honor group, band, and my major in college.

Purpose is affected by identity—If children don't know their strengths, they won't know why they're alive and might actually think they shouldn't have been born. Or if their identity is very narrow, their purpose will be very narrow. If they discover a roadblock to this one thing they think they were created to do, they may not believe there's an alternative route to travel. Identity influences purpose.

Did you have positive purposes when you were young that established healthy thinking that's still relevant today? In my teen years, babysitting was an important purpose for me. I loved helping the parents and getting to know the children. Earning my own spending money was great, too. Practicing my music to earn first-place awards in solo and ensemble contests was also an important purpose during the same years.

Competence is affected by identity—If identity is incomplete and mostly about the negatives, children will doubt they can be competent. They may choose to engage with nothing life-giving. Giving up is easier. I've also seen children so desperate to fill their need for competence that they work on one skill until they master it. But, in the process, they may have developed great stress, lost friends, and lost progress they have made in other areas. Identity influences competence.

Are competencies you began developing in your youth still serving you today? I remind young people that today is related to tomorrow. If they have dreams for their future, they can start working on them today. Did you develop a love of photography and are you now known for the quality of pictures you take? Was curiosity one of your strengths that serves you well as a news reporter? Or, what about the character qualities that formed your competence? Are you grateful you're still brave, responsible, and compassionate today?

Identity matters greatly. If your children have given in to their weaknesses, all the motivation gimmicks in the world won't help. These children don't need stickers, flattery, or easier work and lowered standards. They need a healthy, true, complete identity and many uplifting answers to the question, "Who am I?" Wisely providing these in light of their competence will make a huge difference.

Talk about how identity controls so much of their behavior. You can refer back to the exercise in chapter 2 where they wrote about their strengths, how they developed them, the things they want to improve, and how they're going to do that.

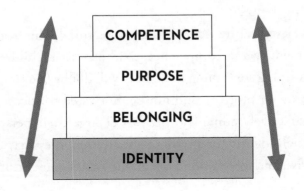

Security: Who can I trust?

Security is the first of the five core needs. Although I understand parents focus on competence because you want your kids to do well and competence is visible, investing time and energy into developing a healthy security will pay huge dividends. It is foundational and influences whether the other four needs will be healthy. And those four needs influence the health of security.

When children know they can trust you, they'll listen longer and with more teachable spirits. When you earn the right to speak into their lives, because of your trustworthy and fair behavior on their behalf, as well as your title of "mom" or "dad," children will be more motivated by you. Your trustworthiness empowers you to influence their identity, belonging, purpose, and competence.

> **Security is the first of the five core needs.**

A lack of healthy security hampers learning. This negatively affects identity and competence. Without trust, children may not risk trying something new. They will doubt your feedback, question your motives, and not be motivated to succeed. You won't effectively convince them to change their perspective about their identity or anything else. Rather, they may choose to be invisible so you don't ask about an assignment or chore they were supposed to do. They'll behave in counterproductive ways. If their security is shaky, they may never develop the competence they could have.

Children feel most secure when they know their parents understand and respect them. This makes their brains feel safe. They can be fully engaged and avoid the fight, flight, or freeze modes.[7] Do you know what confuses and concerns your children? Do you know what they wish they could do better and what they believe will never change? Do you know some of their goals and why they think they're alive? Knowledge like this gives you relational and motivational power.

Modeling trustworthiness and other character traits necessary for establishing trust helps children develop an appropriate level of self-security. In addition to trusting you and more importantly relying on God as the main source of security, they'll be able to trust themselves, as well. This is important so children will be able to be right and to do right even when no one is looking and the burden is heavy. In practical terms, if your children are young, I imagine you look forward to the day when you don't have to hire a babysitter. This will happen when children learn to trust themselves.

Self-security helps children set realistic goals for themselves. They can figure out if they've studied well enough or long enough or if they should ask for help. Security in trustworthy people *and* themselves means they won't place their security in their ability to get everything right. If they do that, they'll crumble when they realize they've made mistakes.

Security allows children to be who they were created to be. They'll wear fewer masks and live with more integrity. Security allows them to choose the friends they want, even if those peers aren't "cool" and others tease them for hanging out with them. Security makes it more likely they'll choose purposes that fit their identity and help friends fulfill their purposes even if they're different from their own. Security means they'll depend on their strengths and not be overwhelmed by weaknesses. Therefore, they'll develop competence.

I'm glad you want your children to be more motivated in the right direction for appropriate reasons and goals. Build up their security. Talk about it.

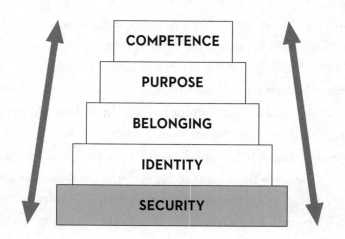

WHAT ABOUT YOU?

Are you still with me? When did you try to meet one of your needs in a way that wasn't good for you? How was it resolved? What did you learn about yourself? Remember, if you or your children have made mistakes regarding meeting these five needs, that's understandable. We all have. We're human! Plus, this might be the first time you're learning about the needs and their relevance. And thankfully, we're covered by God's grace. He is our Redeemer! And He is a Redeemer of all things!

THINGS TO DO

- Identify what you would like a child to be more motivated to do. (Perhaps it's doing a chore without you needing to nag. Maybe it's studying more to improve a math grade. You might have a child who needs to be more compassionate toward a sibling. Maybe you want all your children to be brave and speak up for truth.) Ask yourself how the five core needs are relevant and then talk with the child. Also, remember chapters 2 and 3—Do you and your children need to depend upon new character qualities? What do they need to take off *and* what do they need to put on? Do you need to take anything off and put something on so you can be more supportive and helpful?

Security: Does your son not trust you because you've asked him to improve before and been harsh with him when he hasn't? Is that why your words are not motivating him?

Identity: Has your daughter been told so often that she's average in math that she doesn't believe studying will help?

Belonging: Does your son need to forgive his sibling for teasing him so he can once again demonstrate compassion toward him? Is his anger in his way?

Purpose: Does your daughter mistakenly believe her purpose is just to have fun and that's why doing her chores haven't been her priority?

Competence: Is it possible that your son prefers to be average at all things? Does he like that there's less pressure and less chance of disappointing you?

THINGS TO THINK ABOUT

- In what ways might people confuse wants and needs? What are some dangers of prioritizing meeting wants over needs? Would talking with your children about this be a good idea?

- Each of your children is unique. Think about how you can uniquely meet their different needs.
- Who has helped you meet one or more of your core needs? Pray a prayer of gratitude for them and write them a note. Remind them of how grateful you are for their support.

You rarely have time for everything you want in this life, so you need to make choices. And hopefully your choices can come from a deep sense of who you are.

FRED ROGERS
Host of *Mister Rogers' Neighborhood*[8]

Believe It!—and Thrive

I have good news. When you parent so your children believe three things, their hearts will be impacted and they will be motivated to succeed. This translates into less stress and anxiety and more peace. Who wouldn't want that?

Just three beliefs equip children to find their way around roadblocks. They won't be stopped. They'll see potholes up ahead and wisely negotiate their way around them. They won't get stuck. U-turns won't be as common, but when they're necessary your children won't freak out.

Children who believe these things don't want to be average. They are willing to work for more. They want to be engaged rather than apathetic. They're more likely to choose first-time obedience rather than whining and complaining. They will be resilient.

Children's character will be more Christlike. They'll want to be more others-centered than self-centered. They'll be compassionate, brave and able to stand up for themselves and others. They'll also have reasons to be responsible for their tasks, decisions, and behaviors.

These are like miracle beliefs! What are they?[1]

#1—I Have Value

Making sure children believe they have value is among the most important things you will ever do. This identity issue affects everything including how motivated they'll be and the direction of their motivation. They need to know they have value *now*. They don't have to grow up, become more obedient, or earn an A. They have value because a loving, intentional God created them and Jesus died for them. These realities give everyone value!

If children don't believe in themselves, they don't need to be good at anything. They can be satisfied with Cs, Ds, and Fs. Getting into trouble all the time won't phase them. Memorizing Scripture won't be important. Obedience isn't important. Excellence is irrelevant. Learning is unnecessary. As you read about in the last chapter, what children believe about themselves—identity—influences everything else. They must believe in themselves!

Children who do know they have value are often motivated intrinsically, from the inside. They internally recognize what is good for them and respond accordingly. They'll be more self-motivated. Children who value themselves are also easier to motivate extrinsically, when necessary. They believe in obedience, excellence, learning, and so much more.

What conversations do you need to have with your children about their value? Make the opportunity to talk in specific terms. In addition to the value we all have in Christ, what specific values can you share with them? A friend has always told their first-born daughter that she made them a family. She beams when they remind her of that. What value do your children have?

> Let them know they matter for who they are *and* for what they do.

Does your daughter's joy inspire her grandmother while she's going through a hard time? Did your son's love for music inspire his dad to start playing the guitar again? Does your son's kindness often encourage you at the end of a long day? Let them know they matter for who they are *and* for what they do.

Children need to understand they're important. They're *not* more important than anyone else, but they do matter. If they don't believe this, nothing much matters.

Is it possible that your children aren't motivated in the direction you prefer because they have lost hope for themselves? Have they believed someone who said, "You'll never amount to anything"? Have you been so negative toward them that they now doubt your encouragement? That's real. It happens. We're all human.

#2—Learning Matters

When children believe they have worth, they are more likely to value learning. If they don't have worth, they don't need to learn anything.

It's easier to identify content and lessons that will interest them when you know them and you're in a positive relationship with them. Valuable content, in turn, increases their motivation and reinforces the truth that learning matters. Paying attention to your children more than to their behavior pays great dividends!

If you homeschool, you have the freedom to select content your children will be more motivated to learn and engage with. If you're not homeschooling, you can still guide your children to content they'll care about. Within the teachers' guidelines, you can help children choose topics for papers they have to write and projects they have to complete. For example, for a history course, children could study a person, people group, location, event, or problem that relates to their interests.

Making a good match is only possible when you know your children. You'll know them when you start with their heart. What are their strengths and interests? What's important to them? What goals do they have for the future? What are their dreams? Why do they think they're alive? Remember what I wrote in the last chapter about purpose? When you and your children know why they're alive, you and they can more easily choose and adjust content so they'll be motivated to study. How might science, history, English, art, and other content fit? What interests them? Why might they be willing to persevere?

Kids who value learning will have a much richer and more successful life. Learning is not just important for children in school. Learning matters forever. Here you are learning from reading a book. I'm grateful you know learning changes people and circumstances.

Children who value learning will exhibit many positive character traits, including teachability. This will be true even when they're not convinced that your requests or planned activities are relevant. They'll pay attention anyway because they know they matter and learning matters. These beliefs strengthen children's purpose and give rise to competence.

> *Learning can only happen when*
> *a child is interested.*
> *If he's not interested, it's like throwing*
> *marshmallows at his head and calling it eating.*
> KATRINA GUTLEBEN[2]

#3—My Future Can Be Bright

Believing their future can be bright is the third belief that causes children to be motivated in the right direction. It's

connected to the others. Children who know they have value believe in their future. Because they think of themselves
positively in the present, they project a positive future. This
includes a near future of next month, a distant future of high
school graduation, and a far distant future of meaningful service to the Lord.

Valuing learning also matters for today and tomorrow. If
they lack confidence in their tomorrows and don't believe in
their future, they don't need to bother with today. They don't
need to learn anything. Or be obedient. Or be kind or loving or much of anything else. Apathy and irresponsibility will
serve them well.

Parker's parents, Dmitrius and Andrea, write a vision
statement for Parker each year. Their confidence in him and
his future encourages me. Because they believe in him and his
future, it's more likely he will grow up believing in himself and
his future. They share the statement and things to know about
him, his favorite things, what he's working on, what works,
and what doesn't work with his preschool teachers. This gives
them a great jumpstart on their year together. Parker will learn
more and also believe in his value through their influence.
There are many benefits from parents advocating for their kids.

Here is Dmitrius and Andrea's vision statement for their
precious son with Down syndrome. The entire document they
created is in Appendix C.[3]

"More alike than different." Parker is more like his peers than he is different. He will learn to do everything his typical peers can do, it just might take a bit longer. Our goal for Parker this year is to become acclimated with the learning environment and to grow to love it. We want him to work on developing relationships with his peers and to learn appropriate behaviors for social settings. Our long-term goals for Parker are to be happy and to learn to be an independent adult who contributes to the community in which he lives.

What Do They Value?

When you know what children value, you'll be able to make tasks meaningful and worthwhile and direct them to topics they'll enjoy studying. You'll see why they do or don't want to apply themselves. You'll be able to share more specifics about what they value and why learning is necessary in light of what they hope to accomplish. Knowing what they're interested in will help you motivate them to dream appropriately about their future.

Discerning why children are sometimes very motivated and why sometimes they're not will make all aspects of parenting easier. What is meaningful to them? What do they want to understand better? What do they think about learning? What adjectives do they use to describe themselves? What areas are they interested in or drawn to?

Having answers to questions like these will make your conversations more relevant and appropriate. Your suggestions will be timelier and connected to the issues at hand. Therefore, your children will be motivated in the right direction and successful. All of this increases your credibility.

Starting-stopping. Starting-stopping. Starting again. Stopping again. Stopping or slowing down. It's so frustrating when children behave like this!

Using these two next ideas should help you learn a lot about your children. Although I write about your kids below, as with the change process from chapter 3, use these yourself first to fully understand them. This will help you more confidently use them with your children.

Find Five

"Find Five" is designed to help you know your children's goals. What do they want? What does success look like to them? What will they be motivated to achieve? Choosing meaningful and worthwhile activities will be easier when you know. You'll discover what topics they may want to study. Skills they'll need to master will become clear, too.

Give everyone a piece of paper with this chart on it or ignore the heading and have your kids fold it so they create four squares. Have them write in the four words. Now ask them to list five things in each box that they want in their lifetime. Or, you could use "this school year" or "before Christmas" as the timeframe. Especially young children have a hard time thinking about their entire lifetime. I have used "your lifetime" with children as young as 12 though.

FIVE THINGS IN MY LIFETIME I WANT TO . . .	
BE	DO
HAVE	HELP

This activity can be a fun and revealing one to do as a family. Have everyone do it individually and then come together to compare ideas. Younger children can dictate their ideas to you. Not only will you benefit from learning about your children's top five, but they'll learn a lot about you in a non-threatening way. This can increase your credibility and result in healthier discussions. You might find out you can work on similar goals together. You'll find out how different or similar their goals are to what you dream for them.

You'll also discover what they want that may be unrealistic. One mom told me of a son who wrote down "a baby sister" in the HAVE box. She knew that wouldn't happen. This desire explained a lot of her son's surprising anger. One girl wrote down "happy" in the BE box. Her mom had a careful discussion—not an interrogation—and discovered this was a desire because she was so unhappy at school. She hadn't said anything until this exercise gave her a safe way to open up.

If you need to tell children their goals may not be realistic, you may be able to talk about similar goals to soften the blow a bit. Be ready to demonstrate love and compassion. If you're not supportive, big bubbles can burst and there will be nothing new to replace their ideas with. Pay attention. Maybe they're in denial and they don't have the skills necessary for their goal. Find out if they're willing to work on prerequisite skills and improving themselves. You might have to tell them that you don't have the resources for them to achieve their goal. Discuss and brainstorm what could be done to make the resources available. Again, it might just mean there's a delay until something changes. Or, it might mean different goals are appropriate.

Dreams and goals are vitally important. One sure way to decrease motivation in the right direction is to have children work on goals that aren't realistic. They'll feel like failures and then they *will* fail.

Comparing the four lists is also very relevant. For instance, sometimes what children want to HAVE isn't realistic in light of who they say they want to BE. You will learn a lot that explains their motivation. Is there a lot on their lists related to materialism? Do they want to BE wealthy and HAVE an expensive car? Do they list "travel the world" on their DO list? Or, was the HELP list the easiest for them and is their BE list mostly about their character? Fabulous!

Doing the "Find Five" annually or more often to see how goals and interests have changed is profitable. You could also use it at the beginning of the summer to plan for summer activities that will engage and satisfy everyone in the family.

When will you try this? Do you want to do it first for yourself to see how it feels and what you discover? Then when can you get your kids together to do it? Or, would a one-on-one experience with your most challenging teen be wise? Maybe you could go out to his or her favorite park or coffee shop, share your heart of concern, and then use this as a discussion starter.

Ask Better Questions

Most of today's young people are multi-talented, multi-passionate, and multi-interested. As a result, old questions like "What do you want to do when you grow up?" and "Where do you want to go to college and what will you major in?" aren't effective. They can overwhelm children. Not having answers can frustrate them and concern their grandparents.

Try these questions instead:[4]

- *What problems do you want to help solve?* Children are exposed to the world's brokenness because of the world wide web. As a result, they're oriented toward solving problems. Knowing what they care about can help you plan meaningful lessons so they believe learning matters. Helping them see how they can leave the world a better place through problem solving can deepen their understanding of their value and give them hope for their future.

- *What people groups would you like to serve?* People matter to children, so asking about serving people groups can elicit meaningful responses to help you plug into their interests and concerns.

- *What breaks your heart?* Because of social media posts and "news," children are aware of difficult situations going on locally and around the world. Getting them talking about their heart's responses can help you guide them to optimistic responses and passion.

- *What brings you joy?* In a similar way, knowing causes of joy can help children determine how they want to invest themselves. Joy can help them stay focused and choose tasks and causes they care about.

- *How do you want to live?* I recently met a young person who was interested in serving. He didn't value material things, and had already decided to travel and serve where he could when he was young and not tied down to family or possessions. At the same time, I talked with someone else who had placed a high value on his education because it's relevant to how he wants to leave the world a better place. Knowing your children's values allows you to know how to motivate them better.

WHAT ABOUT YOU?

Do you believe these three beliefs about yourself? Did you believe them when you were a child? When did you learn them? How did you learn them? How would you explain to someone the difference they've made in your life? What steps will you take to make sure your children believe these truths?

THINGS TO DO

- With regard to believing your children have value, talk about what you used to believe and what you currently believe. Ask your children what they believe about their value. Refer back to the lists and drawing they completed after reading chapter 2. What evidence is there that they do or do not value themselves? When you listed things you know about them at the end of chapter 1, what did you include that's relevant?

- Observe your children to look for evidence that they value themselves. Do the ideas on the lists show up? Remember, beliefs cause behavior. Talk with them about what you notice. Ask them questions if you're concerned they may not be valuing themselves as much as you want them to.

- What conversations do you need to have with your children about the value of learning? If you recently emphasized grades and performances more than learning, apologize if you believe it's appropriate. Maybe this is why their curiosity and enthusiasm for new ideas have waned. Appreciate their vulnerability and honesty if they're willing to own their part of the problem. You must help them believe in learning. It takes modeling and many ongoing conversations.

- Talk about how you view the future, how you think your children view it, and how you wish they did. Have you often talked negatively and pessimistically? Apologize if you should. Ask to be forgiven if you believe sin was involved. Appreciate their vulnerability and honesty if they're willing to admit negative views about their tomorrows. You must help them believe in their future. It takes modeling and many ongoing conversations. You might want to go back and skim chapter 4 because the core needs are certainly relevant.

- Write a vision statement for each of your children. If they're old enough, have them write one, too. Compare and talk about anything surprising or concerning.

> **Learning and schoolwork become more important and meaningful when children can use it immediately to benefit others.**

- Use "Find Five" and see if it causes you to think of anything surprising. Make time for the family to do it together. Compare what each of you identifies and make plans based on the results.

- Create opportunities to ask the questions about problems to solve, people to serve, and the others. Help children understand how their answers can drive their motivation. If they don't have well thought-through ideas, make time to talk more about one or more of the questions. Sometimes children will ponder the questions for a while. Two or three days later, they might have more to say.

THINGS TO THINK ABOUT

- In what ways do you celebrate learning and talk well about the future? What about your kids? Do you want to make any changes?

- Learning and schoolwork become more important and meaningful when children can immediately use it. If they can use what they're learning to benefit others, it's even better. Do you need to make any changes in these areas? What? When?

There is a vitality, a life force, an energy, a quickening, that is translated through you into action, and because there is only one of you in all time, this expression is unique.

MARTHA GRAHAM[5]

6

You—a Coach?

How many hats do you wear as a parent? The number of roles you must take on every day can be exhausting. Wardrobe consultant, taxi driver, hair stylist, play-date coordinator, custodian, errand runner, chef, toy repair specialist, lifeguard, personal shopper, driver's teacher, bodyguard, counselor, and dating consultant, just to name a few.

In addition to all these and more, when thinking about how to consistently motivate your children in the right direction, I believe you must be a teacher, coach, cheerleader, and referee—at the right times and in a healthy balance. You currently use all four, yet you might not consistently use the best one at the right time or in the right way. This is what parents in my seminars tell me as they raise their hands to indicate they want to do a better job of using one or more roles effectively.

We've come a long way in understanding what kind of parents call forth maturity, wisdom, and love from their children. (Remember, "parent" means "to bring forth.") I agree with

Angela Duckworth's conclusion that parents who are supportive *and* appropriately demanding raise confident, mature children who are resilient, passionate, and purposeful. These parents know their children and what they're capable of and interested in. They know they need love, limits, and latitude to reach their full potential.[1]

If we were looking for input almost a century ago, we would have trusted John Watson's perspective. He was the chair of psychology at Johns Hopkins University when he wrote his bestselling 1928 parenting guide, *Psychological Care of Infant and Child.* He wrote about how to raise a child "who loses himself in work and play, who quickly learns to overcome the small difficulties in his environment . . . and who finally enters manhood so bulwarked with stable work and emotional habits that no adversity can quite overwhelm him."[2]

Any predictions about his advice?

Never hug and kiss them. Never let them sit in your lap. If you must, kiss them once on the forehead when they say good night. Shake hands with them in the morning. Give them a pat on the head if they have made an extraordinarily good job of a difficult task.[3]

Moreover, Angela Duckworth notes that "Watson further recommends letting children cope with problems on their own 'almost from the moment of birth,' rotating different caregivers to prevent unhealthy attachment to any one adult, and otherwise avoiding the coddling affection that prevents a child from 'conquering the world.'"[4]

The first time I read that, I gasped out loud and then thanked God for how many people have studied to understand what's best for children. This is *not* how to raise secure, healthy, motivated children. When student teaching third graders many years ago, I remember being told by some people not to smile until Thanksgiving. That, too, was not wise. I didn't follow the advice. Looking back, I know it was God impressing upon me that this was not correct.

Jesus celebrated children, even though they were the forgotten generation when He lived on earth. That's why I named my ministry Celebrate Kids. When the disciples asked who among them was the greatest, Jesus called up a child (Matthew 18:1–6). Jesus had a more important purpose than we will ever have, yet He took time to hold and bless children (Mark 10:13–16). His beliefs about children, attitudes toward them, and how He interacted with them are the main reasons I recommend what I do and easily reject Watson's perspective.

I pray you'll be able to teach, coach, cheer, and referee well after reading this chapter. Your children need you to for them to be motivated in the right direction. Also, going back-and-forth between them keeps your heart-tuned relationship healthy, allows your children to use the change process confidently, and helps you meet children's core needs in healthy ways.

Be a Teacher

Children can't do what they don't know how to do. The best motivational strategies and all the stickers in the world won't increase children's short-term and long-term motivation if they're legitimately confused and uncertain. And, as they sometimes tell me, telling and yelling won't help them. You need to teach them.

Be a teacher. Because of our sin nature and the chaotic culture with an anything-goes foundation, obedience and Christlike character are among the most challenging things to get right. We tend to skill and drill the ABCs and 123s, but too many of us state a rule or policy and expect immediate compliance. This isn't the way children learn to do what's right.

Explain what you want your children to do. Include enough details using vivid verbs and descriptive adjectives. Often learning through contrast helps. For example, in age-appropriate ways, talk about what character traits are and what they are not, right and wrong ways to do chores, and neat and sloppy work. This will reinforce the idea that change requires the taking off of what's wrong *and* the putting on of something better.

Show your children what you mean when you can. Save old schoolwork done carefully to contrast it with work you believe is sloppy and carelessly completed. When children are being impatient, call it to their attention using that word.

Explain what they were doing that caused you to call their behavior impatience. Do the same with other qualities. To help them see the value of being organized, you could talk about whether they'd like to set the table if knives, forks, and spoons were all stored in different kitchen drawers.

After you teach and demonstrate, have your children explain what they understand. If you know they get it, hold them accountable, leaving room for individual expression. If they are still confused, teach them to ask specific questions so your additional teaching is directed to what they need to know. (I think you'll love my suggestions about this in chapter 8.)

Do your children seem confused and hesitant? Have you been telling and yelling lately? When and in what ways can you improve and increase your teaching?

Be a Coach

Were you an athlete? If so, you realize coaching is different from teaching. If you weren't, think about what you've seen at athletic competitions, and you can probably predict why I might recommend you coach in addition to teach.

Even more than teachers, coaches break tasks down into bite-size pieces. Doing this makes it easier for children to get started, keep on task, and finish well. Remember, initiative is an important character trait that increases motivation.

Coaches teach, explain, and demonstrate one skill at a

time so players aren't overwhelmed. And, when possible, they allow their athletes to master one skill before adding another.

For example, when I coached middle school girls' basketball, beginners needed to learn how to dribble standing still *and then* while moving down the court. They practiced shooting baskets from a standing position before I had them practice shooting after dribbling to the basket. If they were right-handed, they mastered right-handed layups before I introduced left-handed layups. No matter what you want your children to learn, look for ways to encourage them by breaking down tasks into bite-sized portions, modeling each, and explaining them well.

Good coaches also pay attention to every child to learn about their strengths and weaknesses. They individualize their feedback and coaching—having one child practice dribbling while another practices free throws. Remember your oldest isn't your youngest. A motivation strategy that works for one may not work for the other.

Maybe athletes most appreciate that excellent coaches re-teach without shame or blame. They understand they're asking their athletes to do something complex and new. They don't expect perfection, or anything approaching it, early in the season. They look for progress.

Have you thought of applications to your children? What about "clean your room"? Do you realize how many things are in their room that could be "cleaned"? What about writing an essay? There's word choice, spelling, punctuation, sentence structure, paragraph structure and order, writing style, understanding the content, and more. Getting ready for bed, finishing homework, taking care of their sister . . . I think we'd be hard pressed to think of anything we couldn't break into manageable pieces. Be a coach and explain things well. Then help them put the pieces together for a successful whole.

How can you begin to implement these ideas about coaching? Which child? Which task or quality?

Be a Cheerleader

Cheerleaders provide enthusiastic support throughout the game. Their presence, smiles, physical cheers, and proclamations that athletes can "do it" are significant. But the best cheerleaders in the world cheering exactly the right cheers at the right time won't help an inept team win a game. The team may not even score.

Children need teachers and coaches. Not only that, but children tell me that when you teach and coach them, you earn the right to cheer. They resent parents who cheer "you can do it! You can do it!" when they haven't helped them "do it."

Great cheerleaders pay attention to the game's score so their cheers are realistic. They might begin the game cheering "V-I-C-T-O-R-Y!!" But when the team is down by thirty points in the fourth quarter, they change the cheer. They're still on the sidelines. They still smile and build pyramids. They still cheer, but they might use "Sway to the right, sway to the left, stand up, sit down, fight, fight, fight!"

Children tell me often that it's offensive and upsetting when parents say things like, "You're going to have a great year in math" when there's no evidence they're more capable than they were the previous year. Tears form as they ask me, "Do you think they'll ever accept me even if I keep getting Cs?" Or, more painfully, they ask, "Will they love me even if I keep getting Cs?"

When you're a cheerleader, you get to point out positive choices, attitudes, behaviors, and improvements. You've probably used rewards to do this and to encourage children to maintain their improvements. In a few pages, I'll address how to use rewards well.

Do you need to cheer more consistently? Do you need to cheer some different cheers? With whom? For what?

Be a Referee

There are times when children need you to be a referee. Just like with athletes who are taught and coached well, the more effort you put into teaching and coaching, the less you'll need to referee them. Also, the more you cheer appropriately, the better they'll handle it when you blow the whistle. Your children are human and will forget truth and make mistakes.

That's when you can point out they're over the line, out of bounds, and fouling others.

Pointing out negative decisions, attitudes, and behaviors is something you must do. Maybe punishing children to try to get them to change has been a part of your past. I'll address that choice and why it sometimes works and sometimes doesn't work in just a few pages.

If you don't blow your whistle, your children will continue to make mistakes. If you let them keep repeating the errors, they won't believe they're doing anything wrong or understand they should change. They'll get good at doing the wrong things well. Now change will be more challenging.

You must ref even when you're not in the mood. Remembering your role as a heart-transformer is key. As author and parenting expert Tedd Tripp cautions: "We don't see ourselves as God's agents. We, therefore, correct our children when they irritate us. When their behavior doesn't irritate us, we don't correct them. Thus, our correction is not us rescuing our children from the path of danger; it is rather us airing our frustration."[5]

When you're motivated to ref because it's good for your children, you'll ref when it's necessary even if you're tired, have a lot going on, or would rather not risk ruining your good mood. Then, because your reffing is transforming their hearts for motivation in the right direction, they'll eventually make fewer and fewer errors. You'll need your whistle less.

Your efforts and their efforts will pay off and everyone will be encouraged.

Be courageous. Be the ref now. Are your children fouling others or making mistakes you need to point out? When and how will you?

Use All Four Roles

All four roles matter. When you're concerned with motivating children well, you'll move seamlessly between the roles of teacher, coach, cheerleader, and referee as your children need you. You'll also want to discern which role or roles motivate one child more than another. For example, some children may prefer that you coach rather than cheer. That's true for me—I've always liked being coached. With me, a little bit of cheering goes a long way. Watch and listen for your children's reactions. You can even ask them what they prefer.

Parents often ask me how they can know when to allow children to stop extracurricular activities like piano lessons. Or maybe your issue is a child who was enthusiastic about soccer or karate at the beginning, but no longer is. Your values should inform your decision. For example, my brother and his wife are both musically talented. Music was also important to all our parents. Therefore, their three children all took piano lessons and learned a band instrument, as well. They were all talented, enjoyed band, and made good friends through music.

They were allowed to quit piano lessons when their other instrument became the priority. Then they quit those lessons in high school when they developed different talents and interests. Dave and Deb listened to genuine concerns and intervened, if necessary, but they didn't quit after bad lessons or not being chosen for a concert's solo they thought they deserved. Betsy, Katie, and Andy knew music was something they would do. "Musically talented" is someone they would become.

But the kids weren't required to play in college or choose a college with a marching band, something that was very important to Dave, Debbie, and me. Debbie majored in music and teaching music was her career. Their kids weren't them. They knew and respected that.

If you have taught, coached, cheered, and "reffed" appropriately and kids still want to quit something, it may be time. If they have skills and have been encouraged to enjoy them and use them, but they don't want to, it's okay for interests and skills to not match up. They usually do, but not always. Or, maybe it was just a season of interest. If you force a child to embrace skills in something extracurricular they don't want to do, the damage to your relationship and the trust can be significant. As I've written before, your children may stop believing you and trusting you. They may feel their opinions aren't important to you. As a result, they may stop sharing with you.

Also, many children are too busy today and don't have time to experience new activities. Therefore, they may never discover other passions and strengths. After one to three years of good experiences in drama, music, or sports, they can try something new if they lose interest in their first activity or clearly don't have talent for it. Notice—I'm recommending they go from one activity to another. Not from one activity to video gaming, social media scrolling, or just watching movies. And I'm recommending one to three years. I don't recommend you allow children to quickly quit things you chose for them or they chose for themselves. If you do, they'll never discover that excellence takes time to develop. Their character may be weak. Also, they may not learn to be resilient because they won't need to walk through valleys.

> **Surprising children with grace and mercy is loving them well.**

Use Natural and Logical Consequences

As I wrote above, as a cheerleader, you get to reward your children. As a referee, you're privileged to point out where they need to improve. Maybe you've used punishments to do this.

Rather than using the words "rewards" and "punishments," I recommend using the word "consequences." This small change helps children own their responsibility in changing negative behavior and maintaining positive behavior. Rewards and punishments are things we give children. Consequences are what children earn because of their choices.

Even with young children, you can say, "The consequence for your choice to cheat is that I'll be watching you while you study, and I'll remind your teacher to watch while you take your tests." And, instead of giving a reward when your children do well, you can say, "I'm going to teach you a fun game you can play with your sister as a consequence for choosing to play kindly with her earlier today."

Your children will learn that their behavior matters. It will do your heart good to remember every time you say things like this that you're helping to transform their heart in the right direction as they connect their decisions and the outcomes. There's not always a direct cause/effect relationship between what children do and what happens as a result. When our responses are consistent, though, they'll learn they can depend on us.

Do remember, too, that surprising children with grace and mercy is loving them well. Maybe this is planned inconsistency. Grace and mercy foster empathy and compassion. Your children will also be more inclined to offer grace and mercy to you if you offer it to them. And which parent doesn't need that?

If they ask for a reward or ask how you'll punish them when they disappoint you, you can respond that they're getting what they deserve because of their choices. Remember, it's not up to you; they control your responses. Let them know that when they do the right thing, it's because they love you well. Their love motivates them even when you're not there.

Because you're an experienced parent, you have noticed consequences ("rewards" and "punishments") don't always work. They only work when children want to improve. Are your children willing to do a U-turn and redirect their energies toward healthier choices? Are they willing to put forth the effort to change? If not, even a very large carrot on a stick may not work. I've talked with many parents and children who missed this point and all the motivational gimmicks were for naught.

As I addressed in chapter 3, sometimes children like the negative identity parents want them to change. Maybe they like the power and protection they get from being a bully. They may be afraid to stop for fear they'll be bullied. Maybe they like earning Cs. Your kids may be afraid to do better because they've learned you'll keep expecting that and even more. Have this conversation. Find out if this is the case.

Also, positive consequences you choose only work if they are appealing enough that children want to experience or earn them. The negative ones need to be appalling enough that children want to avoid them. When my parents punished me (rarely, of course!), they sent me to my bedroom. That made sense. It was upstairs, so I was isolated and I had very few toys there. I didn't like it and wanted to avoid this consequence. Today, most children have many fun things in their rooms so sending them there isn't negative and is not something they want to avoid.

Perhaps most importantly of all, children must be able to succeed for consequences to matter. Negative consequences won't give kids the skills they need to be successful. If you keep offering consequences (and bribes and treats as I'll share below) to children who can't perform as you ask, they may feel defeated, unloved, and unaccepted. Sometimes children don't need negative and positive consequences. They need instruction. Be a teacher and coach.

Children need to understand that what they do or don't do causes the consequence. When things go well, the result will be positive consequences. If things don't go well, negative consequences will be in effect. Consequences teach children who to be and who not to be and what to do and what not to do.

Because of technology's reboot function, undo arrow, how easy it is to ex out of games children don't want to finish, and more, they have less understanding about consequences than we might have had at their age. They need to understand life doesn't come with an undo arrow or reboot button. Also, when something breaks, you can't

> Negative consequences won't give kids the skills they need to be successful.

always buy a new one that is better than what you had. Many causes and effects are very real. Today happens and today influences tomorrow. Parent long and strong. Don't give up. Children can learn the cause-effect nature of life.

Natural Consequences

Natural consequences occur naturally—without your influence or intervention. They can be very powerful. For example, on the positive side (i.e., "rewards"), your son may feel joy because he was obedient. Your daughter may experience satisfaction and earn a good grade because she did well on an assignment. Both children may have lasting energy for a long day because they obediently went to sleep on time the night before. These consequences occur naturally without you having to do anything.

Negative natural consequences (i.e., "punishments") include things like your daughter overeating and not feeling well the rest of the night. Your son may be bossy one day and, therefore, experience the consequence of loneliness for a while as friends don't want to play with him. They both may experience anxiety if they forget to study for tests. Their decisions caused these effects.

An advantage of natural consequences is that they occur, and can motivate proper behavior, whether you're aware of what's going on or not. They work when you're not there. When you are there, imagine not having to monitor children's behavior constantly. The key is to stay out of the way of the natural consequence. Let it do its work.

Talking about the consequences your children experience will be essential. Especially young children may need help connecting their decisions and actions to the resulting consequences.

Logical Consequences

When natural consequences are *not* distasteful enough to motivate children to change their attitudes and actions or appealing enough to help children consistently behave in positive ways, you'll need to get directly involved. Use logical consequences (i.e., "rewards" and "punishments") because they logically connect to the negative behavior you're trying to eliminate or the positive behavior you want kids to continue. Positive consequences can get you more of what you want. Negative consequences can get you less of what you don't want.

For example, if you catch your daughter in a lie, a logical consequence could be that you check up on everything she says until she proves she is once again trustworthy. When she declares, "That's not fair!" you can smile and calmly respond like a second-grade teacher I know: "Fair? Fair? When you woke up this morning did someone tell you everything today would be fair? I know children who have no shoes. Think of all the shoes we have! I've seen children who were blind. We can all see. Is that fair? Life isn't fair . . . don't expect it to be." Or you can say, "Your choice to lie means I must check up on you." You can add, "Your choice caused my choice."

If you find out your son has been gaming and not studying in his room like he said he was, and the natural consequence of low grades isn't changing his behavior, you can institute a logical consequence or two. You could require that he study in the room you're in so he can't be gaming on his device. You could ask teachers to report daily on how he's doing. You could delete games/apps that were hardest for him to be self-controlled with. These decisions make sense because they should result in more studying and higher grades. You can say something like, "You chose my decisions by deciding to not study in your room. We thought we could trust you. You can earn the right to prove yourself trustworthy again by your current choices. That includes your attitude."

If your daughter consistently leaves her bike outside at the end of the day rather than putting it in the garage as you've asked her to do, a logical consequence is appropriate. For instance, she could lose the privilege of riding for a day or two. If she accuses you of being mean, you need to remind her, "Your choice to not take care of your bike means I couldn't trust you to use it today."

Choose positive logical consequences to teach children what to do rather than what not to do—what behaviors to continue. This is an important part of your role as cheerleader. When natural consequences haven't worked, logical ones will help children see the benefit of positive behaviors, supply extra motivation, and make it more certain they'll continue down the right path long enough to establish a new habit.

Logical consequences are effective because they're related to the task or behavior your children are working on. For example, if they cooperate well for several days in a row, buy them or teach them a new game they can play together. Or, if you're pleased with your daughter's growing independence and you want to encourage and thank her, you could purchase something small she can enjoy when alone. Occasional uses of logical consequences like this can significantly improve motivation. But pay close attention to my cautions below.

Use Bribes and Treats

A bribe is not a consequence. A bribe is something you offer children to get them to do what you need them to do. A consequence is what they get for doing it.

Bribes have their place, but limiting their use is essential. Sometimes you may need to bribe your children to help them initiate new attitudes or actions or to stop negative ones. This is especially true when they don't believe they're capable or they just don't want to do it. Potty training comes to mind. Bribery works because young children don't know they're capable of using a toilet and they don't want to.

Don't bribe unless you believe it's the only way to get children moving in the right direction—away from what you don't want for them and toward the things you do want for them. Bribing can suggest you don't think your children can do it on their own. Therefore, bribes can lower self-confidence and self-motivation, two qualities you want your children to exhibit. Use bribes only when nothing else has worked.[6]

Use the bribe only as long as necessary. Once children begin behaving in the ways you want, gradually withdraw the bribe so they discover they're capable of the new behavior. In other words, they did not do what you asked them to only because of the "carrot on the stick." They did it because they're capable. Eventually, withdraw the bribe, use logical positive consequences, if necessary, and then rely on natural consequences to help children maintain their right choices.

What About Treats?

It's sometimes fun and appropriate to surprise children with treats. Movie tickets, ice cream cones, bike rides with Dad, quick stops at the library, homemade lemonade, playing a game, and any number of things can motivate children. These aren't consequences because they're not directly related to the behavior you're working on, but they're beneficial. They communicate, "I know you've been working hard" and "Next week can be better."

Three Categories to Use

Get creative when choosing consequences, bribes, and treats. Variety will serve you well. These basic categories may help you think through your situation.

Time

Taking time away from a favorite activity, canceling it, or adding time to an unpleasant activity can be effective negative consequences and bribes (e.g., because you wasted time while studying you won't be able to Facetime with Joshua tonight; if you don't get your chores finished in the next hour, you'll have to spend time on them tomorrow which means less time at the dog park).

Adding time to a favorite activity, taking time away from an unpleasant activity, or canceling it can be effective positive consequences, bribes, or treats (e.g., if you finish your assignment in 10 minutes we'll have time to make cupcakes together; because you cooperated well tonight you may stay up later and play one more game).

People

People can serve as consequences and bribes (e.g., more or less time with certain friends, time with or without siblings, one-on-one time with Dad or Mom, alone time).

Things

Any number of things can serve as consequences, bribes, and treats (e.g., because you worked hard on your reading and discovered it can be enjoyable, we'll go to the bookstore tonight and you may choose a book; because you have not been a gracious loser lately, your mom and I are going to play a game with just your brothers).

NATURAL CONSEQUENCES	Naturally occur because of children's choices.
	Children earn these; they are a result of their choices.
	Parents don't give them.
	Parents don't need to be present or involved.
LOGICAL CONSEQUENCES	Logically occur because of children's choices.
	Children earn these; they are a result of their choices.
	They are related to the issue at hand.
	Parents choose these and give them to children.

POSITIVE CONSEQUENCES	Designed to get more of what you want. They work when children want to earn them. Often called "rewards."
NEGATIVE CONSEQUENCES	Designed to get less of what you don't want. They work when children don't want them. Often called "punishments."
BRIBES	Offered to children to motivate them to do something unpleasant or that they don't know they can do. They do not need to be related to the issue at hand. Parents choose them and give them to children.
TREATS	A surprise to encourage children. They do not need to be related to the issue at hand. Parents choose them and give them to children.

Use Consequences, Bribes, and Treats Effectively

Keep the following in mind and you'll be successful.

Use Them If They're Necessary

When children already demonstrate some internal, intrinsic motivation for an attitude, action, task, and the like, let the natural consequences that occur encourage them. Children who are intrinsically motivated don't need someone to motivate them. They have all they need internally and, gratefully, will be good even when you're not there. They are self-starters, using the character quality of initiative. They can follow through with appropriate effort, diligence, and perseverance to finish their chores, to study, to be obedient, and to treat others with respect.

Don't get in the way of intrinsically motivated kids. Using consequences can decrease the intrinsic motivation you want them to rely on. You can acknowledge that they're doing well. Saying "thank you" can be very powerful. Occasionally and spontaneously offering a treat of some kind will show them you're aware of their wise decisions.

Ideally children become their own GPS and redirect themselves toward things that are healthy and good for them. As they mature, they decide to avoid potholes they see up ahead. They figure out how to avoid common barriers to progress.

They discover they can choose success rather than failure, learning instead of forgetting, and obedience not disobedience, positive character not negative, and love not hate.

Make Them Personal

When you think about what logical consequences, treats, and bribes might motivate and help your children, think about who they are. The information in chapter 10 about how your children are smart will intrigue and help you. Remember what I wrote back in chapter 4. Knowing your children's identity and making sure they know themselves well is significant for many reasons. This is one of them.

Not only do you want consequences to match the behavior you're working on, but you also want them to fit the child. This makes it more likely they'll have motivational power. For example, if your daughter enjoys being creative, take her to a craft store and enjoy looking around together. If your son has argued rather than being respectful and you could choose one of several things to take away as a negative consequence, choose what seems most important to him in the moment because there will be more "pain." Perhaps it's his device so he can't play his favorite game.

You may want to ask your children what they think would help them. Some children have very realistic ideas. Because of the buy-in, using one of their ideas will often work better than using one of your ideas. Other children will have very unrealistic ideas, like a trip to Disneyland for a straight-A report card. This option will give you something to talk about!

Use Both Positive and Negative Consequences

Children will respond best when you use a good balance of positive and negative consequences (i.e., "rewards" and "punishments"). When you're working hard to help them make progress, there may be a need for some negative consequences to be in effect. You'll need to be a referee, correcting a lot. But you'll come across as critical if you don't also point out things they're doing well.

Think about yourself. Do you enjoy being with people who only point out what you're doing wrong and where you could improve? They're negative and they think this will help you change. How do you feel about yourself and them? Are you motivated to take risks? To try again? I doubt it.

Your children are no different. There's always something good going on. Always! When you choose to see it and draw it to their attention, your relationship will be healthy. They'll trust you. Remember from chapter 3, that without security you are less likely to influence them positively. Also, we all use our strengths to compensate for weaknesses and to improve our weaknesses. Your children must know what they're doing well. It motivates them!

Withdraw Them Appropriately

Always give natural consequences a chance to work. It can take time for the negative effects to motivate your children to change. While you wait, and while your kids are still learning why to be compassionate toward their neighbor, how to do a chore, or how to use a memorization strategy, coach them more. Reteach without blame or shame. Offer some cheers and refereeing. If progress is slow with all of this, then use logical consequences. If that's not enough, bribe them to jumpstart progress. Don't bribe before there's proof you need to. Don't implement positive or negative logical consequences until you need to.

Gradually and systematically withdrawing the bribes and positive consequences is essential. You must make sure children don't become dependent upon the "prizes." Instead, they must understand they're making changes because they're capable of doing what's right. Also, when you think it's true, let them know it's their love for Christ and you that's compelling them to change. This is why we start with the heart. (Can you imagine giving your children M&Ms every time they go to the bathroom successfully long after they learned how? No, of course not. Can you also see how they might not have been successful if you would have stopped offering M&Ms cold turkey before they had mastered the skill?)

For instance, you may award your daughter one point for

every five minutes of focused attention while she's working on her lessons. When she accumulates ten points, she can choose to do whatever activity she wants for ten minutes. This positive consequence can help her value time more. Eventually, after she is consistently successful, you'll want to make it harder for her to earn her point. For instance, you could have her pay attention for eight minutes and then ten minutes to earn one point. And maybe she doesn't get free time until she's accumulated fifteen points and then twenty. Eventually you'll stop awarding points regularly.

If your daughter complains that she wants the points and a chance to earn free time, confidently tell her she doesn't need them anymore because she has learned to focus on her schoolwork. Teach her how pleased you are with her choice to honor you and her use of time. Use your words well to keep her motivated.

To encourage your daughter to maintain her ability to focus, use random logical consequences. Random attention works best to instill long-term motivation.[7] Surprising children reinforces the natural consequences that have been in place this whole time. If your children feel ignored after being successful for a while, they may revert to their old ways to get your attention. Random support helps to maintain proper performance. Remember, too, that reteaching and coaching may be necessary.

You can do this!

WHAT ABOUT YOU?

Do you see God relating to you as a teacher, coach, cheer-leader, and referee? In what ways and when? How does that make you feel? Can you think of a time when you did something wrong and felt like you got away with it? What natural

Parent long and strong.

consequences occurred? Do you have the kind of relationship with your kids that gives them the freedom to tell you if they did something wrong and thought they got away with it? Why or why not? Confession and forgiveness are good for the soul.

THINGS TO DO

- Let's apply the four roles first to developing healthy character—it's such an important part of the heart. You could choose to emphasize the character quali-ties from chapter 2 or others from Appendix A. Or begin with the character quality you wish your daughter would use consistently (e.g., fairness, gen-tleness, politeness). You'll want to have a long-term view of instilling character into your children. Re-member—parent long and strong. Come back to this idea regularly.

- Use questions like these to learn how to support your daughter and your other children: What is preventing success? Do you need to teach more rather than just tell? Do you need to coach by breaking down the quality into observable elements and helping her see how it's related to other traits? Do you need to cheer more or change the cheer you've been using so she is more hopeful? What about refereeing? Does she need to understand more about what's wrong? Implement some changes in your approach and look for changes.

- Choose one behavior you wish your son would master (e.g., practicing piano without being nagged, putting his dirty and clean clothes where they belong, honoring your curfew). List positive and negative natural consequences that occur for him and make an effort to point out how these are in effect. List positive and negative logical consequences you can use if he doesn't make progress. Think about time, people, and things. If you think you may need to bribe him to make quicker progress and eventually master the task, list options. Do the same for treats. Make a list of those that fit him well. Do this for one or two other behaviors, too, for this son and for other kids so you're ready to act when you need to.

• Are you aware if a child is too dependent on your help and needs to develop intrinsic motivation? How can you transfer responsibility to your child by designing a system to decrease your use of logical consequences? Write out a plan to systematically and gradually withdraw their use so your child can independently be successful even when you're not there.

THINGS TO THINK ABOUT

• In what ways has the way you were parented influenced your parenting style? Did a parent or anyone else who influenced you lean toward believing any part of John Watson's advice? If so, and especially if you think it's still influencing you, what kind of processing will benefit you and your children? Would praying be wise? Talking to anyone? Forgiving?

• What role is easiest for you? Referee? Cheerleader? Coach? Teacher? How might this be influencing how you use them? Are any changes in order?

• Can you picture yourself telling your children or other parents why you're using the word "consequence" instead of "reward" and "punishment"? How would you explain the benefit of this change?

The more you sweat in practice,
the less you bleed in battle.

UNKNOWN

How to Communicate
So Your Children Will Hear You

Which is better?

"Be on time!"

"Don't be late!"

Do you hear the difference? Which one is positive? "Be on time" communicates "I believe you're capable of this." It's more hopeful. It's about what you want your children to do. "Don't be late" reminds them of how they've frustrated you.

When you communicate in ways your children will hear you, you can influence them in the right direction. When you're honest, they will trust you and you will meet their need for security. If you use other healthy character traits as you talk and listen, they'll be more motivated and more able to develop Christlike character. When you communicate based on hope in them and their future, they will want to listen. Belonging will be solid and your relationship will be healthy.

Whether you're teaching, coaching, cheering, or refereeing,

children benefit when you choose to be *optimistic, positive, encouraging,* and *enthusiastic.* Admit it. Even as an adult, wouldn't you rather spend time with and listen to people who communicate in these ways? Isn't being motivated in the right direction more likely?

These four communication styles will also make resiliency more likely both for you and your children. You can't afford to give up or let hard days or hard children defeat you. When you choose to be optimistic, positive, encouraging, and enthusiastic, staying down is less likely. You'll bounce back and move forward. So will your kids. When your communication is founded on these four styles, children will believe you when you declare that mistakes happen when we learn. They'll know their mistakes don't define or defeat them. They'll know making mistakes and failing are two different things. They'll believe failure isn't final, and failure isn't fatal.

> You can't afford to give up or let hard days or hard children defeat you.

Be Optimistic

Optimism is important when motivating others because of its observational and communication power. When you're optimistic, you expect things to go well. You're oriented to success and expect favorable outcomes. Optimists look first for what's right. They see what's wrong only if it's necessary. These are among the reasons optimism protects children against depression and anxiety.[1]

Optimists communicate joy and hope through smiles, eye contact, welcoming body language, and truth. When optimistic, you don't panic when children spill their milk and make spelling mistakes. And you don't communicate the expectation that they'll repeat these troubles the next day. That's a key point of being optimistic and one that children greatly appreciate. Just as God's mercies are new every morning, yours can be, too.

Your optimism also means you'll explain things without resenting children's need for the explanation. When you communicate well, you expect your teaching to work and your children to learn. You're positive toward yourself and them because you expect they will "get it." You understand learning new things takes time and mistakes may occur. That doesn't mean they're "bad" or "dumb." It doesn't mean you're ineffective or "a bad parent."

Be optimistic at all times, but be careful expressing it when children don't have the skills to succeed at a task at hand. Even if they have the skills, but believe they can't succeed, be careful. This is when you need to change the cheer. If you don't, children will decide they can't trust you. They won't be able to meet their need for security in you. The quality of your relationship will be at risk. Observe carefully. "I think you can. I think you can" doesn't always work.

Be Positive

Positive people are optimists who carry their expectation that things will go well to the language they use. When being positive, you carefully choose the tone and words you use when communicating. This is very important for parents who want children to change around.

Tell them what to do, not what not to do

Being positive motivates parents to talk more about what you want than the negative behavior you don't want. Positive parents use words to direct children's behavior to what is good. This is efficient, instructive, and will build trust.

For example, "Don't be so loud!" and "Use your inside voice" say about the same thing. The first tells children what *not* to do; the second tells them what *to* do. Which one will motivate your children in the right direction?

"Stop being so rough with the dog" vs. "Be gentle when you pet the dog."

"I'm sick of your laziness! You're not helping out around here at all!" vs. "It's time to help us put the winter stuff away in the garage and get out our bikes and outdoor toys we enjoy using in the spring. It won't take long if we each do our part."

Other examples of positive and negative communication include phrases like, "Please remember" and "Don't forget." Which one more easily reminds children of times when they've disappointed you in the past? "Don't forget." It can solidify the identity of "I'm forgetful." It can discourage children. They may think, "I'll forget again. I always do!"

"Don't forget to clean your bathroom this morning." vs. "Remember to clean your bathroom this morning."

"Don't forget to call Mrs. Kyle." vs. "Remember to call Mrs. Kyle and let her know about the babysitting job."

"Don't be late for soccer practice." vs. "Be on time for soccer practice."

"Don't be late again!" vs. "I know you can be on time tonight."

Years ago, when going out to eat in Denver, I became convinced that what appear to be minor differences in phrases like these aren't minor at all. A group of us were dropped off at a restaurant while our host parked the car. Walking in, we were greeted by a sign at the hostess station that stated, "We will not seat incomplete parties." There are two negatives in that sentence! We didn't feel welcome even though our group would only be incomplete for a few minutes.

The very next night, our host again dropped us off, but at a different restaurant. This time, the sign read, "We will gladly seat complete parties." We all noticed the difference.

It communicates the same truth as the other sign, but in a welcoming, affirming, and positive way.

Use helpful, non-bullying language

When you need to point out children's weaknesses and correct them, your choice of words matters. For example, calling children "fat" isn't appropriate. "Overweight" might be an accurate word. "Needs more exercise" and "would benefit from making smarter food choices" might both be accurate. It doesn't do children any good to call them "fat." That's a word children use on the playground when wanting to put children down. They shouldn't hear this in your home.

Plus, the word "fat" doesn't motivate children to change. I know in my desire to lose weight, the words I assign myself matter greatly. People who think of themselves as fat might overeat and not think much about whether the food they choose to eat is healthy. Even when I have thought of myself as "overweight," I would sometimes look at a restaurant's menu and choose unhealthy food, thinking "I'm already overweight so it doesn't matter."

The identity "I'm making healthier food choices" matters to me. I started with "I can make healthier food choices" and then "I will make healthier food choices." Now, "I'm making better choices." Once true, it's easier to maintain the behavior.

What are some examples from your life or a child's life?

When talking with a group of boys, one admitted his mom called him a "lazy slob." Others chimed in that they've been told that, too. The first boy told me he didn't understand what "lazy" and "slob" had to do with each other or what his mom meant. What's an accurate and kinder way this mom could have communicated her concern?

Are there any negative words you could stop using? Maybe you started in times of great frustration when you felt hopeless. I get it. You can change. Your children will be more resilient if you do. Plan ahead and think of better words or phrases to communicate in a helpful, more positive way. Negative words children have shared with me, sometimes with tears, include stupid, dumb, good-for-nothing, a waste, high maintenance, and disgusting.

I'll never forget one of the girls who said she was called "disgusting." She admitted that her parents called the thing she was doing disgusting (e.g., playing with her food, telling a weird joke, wearing dirty clothes) and not her directly. But she said that didn't matter. She still felt they were calling *her* disgusting.

Reflect your hope for the future

When you're positive, you'll hear children's negative statements about the past and know how to quickly orient them to the future.

For example, your son might get frustrated while reading out loud with you and proclaim, "I am not good at this!" You can respond, "That was a challenging section today. You will learn." This is much more motivating than asking, "Why didn't you do better?" Or, "What are you going to do about it?" Your son might look at his finished work and comment, "I'm great at this. It was so easy!" Your comeback could be, "Do you remember it didn't use to be easy? You practiced and had a great attitude. I'm proud of you!" These comments reinforce your son's smart decisions and remind him of behaviors he can apply to things that challenge him now.

Be Encouraging

If you're like me, you want to spend time with optimistic, positive people who encourage you. So do your children. If you want your relationship to be solid and to have more influence over them, be an optimist and not a pessimist, be positive and not negative, and be encouraging and not discouraging.

When you are optimistic and positive you can encourage your children. They will be inspired and confident. They will want to be with you. They'll more regularly seek your opinion and care about your input. They'll admit when they struggle and ask for help rather than lying and hiding from you. They'll willingly risk learning new things when there's no guarantee they'll do well initially.

These behaviors are possible because your children will be brave and courageous due to your encouragement. Have you ever noticed that the base word of "encourage" is "courage"? When you encourage your children, you give them courage. They will be brave. Avoid discouraging your children because it means you have stolen their courage.

We need kids to be brave! It's rooted in encouragement. Children who have never taken piano lessons need to be courageous. Children who play soccer for the first time need to be courageous. The first weeks of fourth grade, physics, and marching band all require courage because risks abound.

If you discourage children by always comparing them to others, talking about how hard things might be, talking first about their mistakes, and always using a demeaning tone of voice, they'll not achieve as much as they might have. No courage = no learning.

Children are encouraged by different things, so observe carefully. Choosing the best role for the circumstances motivates them. So do logical consequences and treats that fit them. Some are encouraged by more instruction; some by the right cheers. Some are encouraged by parties; some may be overwhelmed by all the attention. Some are encouraged as you look over their shoulder when they practice; some want to call for you only when they need you.

> **Children are encouraged by different things, so observe carefully.**

You'll more likely encourage children when pointing out what they do right than what they do wrong. Or, at least do both. It can depend if the subject is new, if they applied themselves when doing their work, and other factors. But, when your goal is to encourage, it's almost always wisest to emphasize strengths and what's right.

For instance, if your daughter's graded math paper has "-3" at the top, she might show it to you with, "Look Mom, I only got 3 wrong!" Imagine if that same paper had "+22" at the top. Now she says, "Look Mom, I got 22 right!"

If your son is upset with a grade or performance, listen as he processes his disappointment. Interact with him and respond with compassion. Don't immediately offer solutions. There's definitely a time and place for that. But, when your goal is to encourage him so he won't give up and he'll willingly risk again, you want to talk about strengths first.

When you can, ask your son what he is happy about. What did he do well or better than the last time? Maybe he made spelling mistakes in his story, but he remembered to choose vivid adjectives. When talking about his soccer game, maybe he'll talk about missing the goal when kicking to score, but he recognizes he ran more without being winded. In both cases, when he's ready, talk about his challenges and how to improve in the future.

Be Enthusiastic

Children need you to be enthusiastic for them. They benefit when you care about what they're interested in, what they're doing, who they're becoming, and more. Enthusiasm is defined as "lively interest." It's the opposite of indifference, and it's essential if you want your heart and your children's hearts to be bound together.

Indifference might be one of the saddest things children experience. If you've been indifferent, or they think you've been indifferent, you'll have to earn their trust. Busyness, fatigue, your own challenges, constant frustration with your children, and other factors possibly caused you to distance yourself from one or more of your children. I understand.

I pray your reasons do not continue being excuses to be indifferent. Have grace for yourself and use the truths here to increase your enthusiasm. I'm grateful you're reading this book and are aware that change is necessary for your children to be motivated for more.

If you drastically change your communication style and suddenly become very interested and involved, children may be suspicious. For instance, if you've only been a teacher and referee and all of a sudden you become a cheerleader, they may push back and doubt you. Talk about your choice to re-engage and make gradual changes to be enthusiastically on their side. Don't let your enthusiasm overpower you or them.

Guard yourself to make sure you tell the truth and don't exaggerate your hope for your children. Your desire that they do well and now know you're enthusiastic can cause you to make statements that backfire. Sometimes it's possible to become too enthusiastic. I hear about this too often from children. This example is from a seventh grader:

> "My dad said, 'I know you can earn an A. You'll do it this year.' But, I've never earned more than a B and that was mostly luck. I don't think my dad even knows me. He hasn't been paying attention. Math is really hard for me. I'm going to disappoint him bad this year. He wants me to get an A! I don't know what to do."

On the inside, I think this child is screaming, "Will you not accept me for the B student God created me to be?" I know this dad just wants to motivate his son. But he needs to change his cheer.

The Engine That Said Yes

In *The Little Engine That Could*,[2] the toys are looking for a way to get to children's houses for Christmas. When they ask a little blue engine that comes chugging along, she says yes! The whole story is a beautiful description of optimism, kindness, and compassion. The blue engine feels sorry for the toys and agrees to take them where they need to go.

These qualities go hand-in-hand. If you want children to be optimistic, teach them to be resilient. If you want them to recover quickly from defeat, be optimistic about them and when you interact with them.

Optimism is more than happy talk. It's critical to resiliency. Compassion motivates. Purpose motivates. Prioritize them in yourself and your children.

The story of the little engine also reminds us that, despite the lies of our technological age, some things are hard. Some things take a long time. Life isn't always easy and automatic. We see the blue engine pulling and tugging and "slowly, slowly, slowly" starting off. Always remind your children that desire and effort matter greatly.

> Always remind your children that desire and effort matter greatly.

And when we're encouraged by those who are optimistic, positive, enthusiastic, and resilient—we can discover our internal strengths. So can our kids. Just ask the engine, who discovered that she *could* make it over the mountain!

Starting with the heart will make these qualities more likely in you. Starting with the heart will also cause you to know your kids. You'll know when to teach and when coaching will support them well. You'll know when to cheer, what cheer they'll respond well to, and when to change the cheer. You'll know how to ref in their current situation so they'll still be secure in you.

Cheering, "I think you can. I think you can." when you don't believe your children actually can do it—whatever the "it" is—will damage trust and security. Allowing your children to cheer for themselves when you yourself think they can't is also unloving.

Being a cheerleader is important, but it won't take the place of a teacher and coach. Being optimistic, positive, encouraging, and enthusiastic motivates children. but these communication styles must support real skills and important truths.

WHAT ABOUT YOU?

In your hard work of parenting, do you have friends who are optimistic, positive, encouraging, and enthusiastic for you and about you? Do you recognize what help you need to stay strong and parent long with your children? What about finding a mentor parent with older children who can give you a heads up and ideas about what's coming next with your kids? Mentors don't have to have be perfect parents or have perfect kids. They must be learners, on the way, just like you.

THINGS TO DO

- Purchase or borrow a copy of *The Little Engine That Could*. Read it to yourself, looking for lessons for yourself. Enjoy reading it to your children. Depending on their age and current level of motivation, either share lessons with them or ask them what they hear and see that's relevant. Use this as a bonding experience. Come back to the book often.

- Are you someone who is naturally optimistic, positive, encouraging, and enthusiastic? Keep at it! If you're not, what could help you change? What do you need to take off and how might you renew your mind? Resting, having quiet time with God, spending time with optimistic people, choosing to acknowledge and celebrate your strengths, having fun with your children? Do what it takes. You're worth it and so are your children.

- Challenge your family to stop being negative and complaining. Try to go an entire day without verbalizing a complaint. Choose to verbalize one compliment or thank-you statement instead. Try to go two days in a row. Then three. Then four . . . Talk about how everyone is doing and feeling.

- You and your children might enjoy working to stand an egg upright as a way of talking about the value of optimism and positive talk.[3] As your children know, eggs naturally lie on their long axis. But an egg can stand up vertically with the use of salt.

   You could talk about wanting to lie down when things don't go well. We might have an "I give up" response to parts of life. With positive beliefs and talk (salt), we're more inclined to stand up and face the world.

   On its own, the egg can't stay upright. It won't work. But it will stand in a pile of salt as you gently shift the egg back and forth until it feels stable in its upright position. It won't easily stand in the salt; the pile has to be just right and you have to work at it. But it will work. Use that analogy that salt is like optimism and positive talk. They both support us in our desires to grow and learn new things.

THINGS TO THINK ABOUT

- How might you let your kids know that you haven't been the greatest communicator and you want to get better? What are the advantages of letting them know you'll be working on this and want their help?

- How can you encourage your children to express optimism toward their siblings? Are there any activities you could plan this weekend or games you could play that would allow you to easily talk about being positive, encouraging, and enthusiastic for each other?

- Would you describe your parents and others who influenced you in your childhood and young-adult years as being optimistic, positive, encouraging, and enthusiastic? If not, have their communication styles affected you? If they have, what can you do to overcome anything negative?

*Hope deferred makes the heart sick, but a
desire fulfilled is a tree of life.*

PROVERBS 13:12

8

Listening Longer
and Other Essentials of
Good Communication

As you think back over the past few days, can you identify moments of ideal communication with anybody? What about times with you and your kids when you know you said "this" and they thought you said "that"? This happens to all of us. It demotivates, that's for sure.

Maybe your quick temper got the best of you. Maybe you became frustrated when your son said he was confused. You thought you carefully explained things, but he said he didn't remember, got frustrated, and then yelled. You yelled back.

Have grace for yourself—have grace for your children. No one is perfect and motivation is more complex than you probably thought it was. As I frequently say, you didn't understand some of this yesterday. No shame. No blame. I hope and pray these ideas are giving you hope for your tomorrows.

The communication styles I addressed in the last chapter

serve as a foundation to the ideas I present here and in the next chapter. There you'll learn about the art of complimenting and correcting. These specific reasons for communicating are also very powerful.

Listen Longer

Listening longer can prevent many communication problems. Of course, to make listening longer possible, your children have to talk. If you want them to share with you when they're older, listen to them when they're young. Listen to their stories and interact about the things on their minds. Be interested.

Teens tell me they resent parents' interest "all of a sudden" when they appeared apathetic earlier. For instance, I've heard, "I don't know what they think happened now that I'm 13. I'm the same kid. Why do they all of a sudden need to know everything? Why don't they trust me?" If you have preteens and teens and this is your situation, own it. Apologize for what looked like a lack of interest when they were young. Ask to be forgiven.

The next time your children come to you and share something that concerns you, listen longer to get more information before you jump to conclusions, start to problem solve, and try to fix things. "Read" their body language and look under the surface for emotions.

Paying attention to children's feelings is natural for parents who start with the heart. It's essential for keeping your relationship solid and for establishing security in each other. Also, talk about your children's emotions because their ability to manage negative emotions is necessary if they're going to be resilient. Talking about emotions also strengthens their impulse-control muscles.[1]

Ask for details about their feelings, if you must, but don't interrogate them. You probably don't mean to interrogate them, but it's a word children use when telling me what frustrates them about their parents. Your questions can feel intrusive and as if you don't trust them. They may clam up and offer you very little. Your questions may decrease motivation and cooperation.

Although I know your heart is to prevent problems and solve the ones that occur, if you quickly make

> Ask for details about your children's feelings, but don't interrogate them.

children feel like problems you're trying to solve or projects you're trying to finish, discouragement can set in.[2] Children tell me it's one of the things that makes them feel unloved and like they can't get anything right. Anger can be quick. Also, children will become more resilient when you and their teachers don't try to fix all their problems. They have to learn to wrestle with everyday challenges so they can handle major disappointments later. Remember what I wrote in chapter 1. Resiliency is a key to children's motivation.

Your children won't learn as much if you do all the thinking for them through your interrogation and reactions to their ideas. And don't assume they necessarily want you to help them figure things out when they share something with you. I've learned it's wise to ask something like, "Would you like my thoughts or questions or did you just need to hear yourself talk about it?" They might not be ready for your reactions yet, but they may ask for them later.

Don't be offended. It's not about you being helpful in this moment. It's about your children being heard. Wait for them to be ready, and they'll be more motivated to hear your ideas.

When your children appear to be finished talking, you can say, "And . . . ?" with a tone of voice that invites more information. If they respond by whining, "What?" just say you wonder if they have more to share. Add that you want to understand.

You can also use "Keep talking" and "Tell me more." Then wait and be quiet for a while. These open-ended ideas allow kids to share what they want rather than to answer your question. You will often get valuable information by inviting rather than directing.

Children tell me they prefer talking about tough stuff in the dark at bedtime and while you're driving. They don't want to look into your eyes when they know they may hurt your heart. They also appreciate that you're captured in the car and can't leave if the conversation gets stressful. They can't leave either—and that's to your advantage.

Boys almost always talk more when they're busy doing something.[3] If you want to know what's going on in your son's life, you could weed the garden together, go through his workout clothes to decide which ones don't fit anymore, or go walk the aisles at a store he enjoys. While you're busy, he may begin talking spontaneously about more important things. You'll be able to listen longer because he'll talk more.

Correct Lies Children Tell About Themselves

Lying to ourselves and others is never healthy. It changes identity. If you look back to chapter 3, you'll remember the importance of identity. Like the other core needs, it influences competence and whether your children will accept your motivational help. Identity controls behavior. Who we think we are is who we will be. This is why you cannot let your children lie to themselves.

If you overhear your daughter mumble, "I'm so stupid!" while looking at an assignment, you need to talk about that. This is especially true if she knows you heard her. If she knows you did and you don't correct her, what happens? She'll decide you agree with her. Now, as you offer to help her and to improve her motivation, she'll think you're doing it because she's stupid.

If there are others around, you may need to wait to have the discussion, but as soon as you can, talk about what she said. Or, you may want to do it immediately so her friends and family know you disagree with her. Admit you heard it and you were surprised. Ask her for evidence that she is stupid. She won't have any! She might say it's hard, but that doesn't mean she's stupid. Maybe she wasn't listening to instructions and that's why she feels stupid. That's evidence of "not listening," but not evidence of being stupid. Or, maybe she feels stupid because that task is new. It might mean she'll have to be diligent. Encourage her to speak the truth.

If your son earns a low grade on a project and proclaims he is stupid, the teacher is unfair, or he can't do anything right, talk about his conclusion. Let him know you recognize his frustration and disappointment. Then ask him to defend his statements. He won't be able to. He might have been careless—that's not the same as stupid. Maybe he forgot the due date and had to hurry to complete the project. Maybe he didn't ask the teacher to clarify something. Neither is the same as being stupid.

Ask him what makes him think the teacher was unfair. If there's anything legitimate, ask him if he'll talk with the teacher and whether he would like your help. If he's whining and trying to assign blame that's not the teacher's, talk about it.

To confront the lie that "I can't do anything right," make

a list of right and good things your son has done lately. At the conclusion of this discussion, have your son state the truth about the project and the grade he earned.

Let me briefly share another type of lie that can mess with motivation. I used to think and maybe verbalize to friends, "I'm going to clean my house this weekend." Then, when I didn't "clean my house" I was discouraged at the end of the weekend. I was lying to myself. I can't clean my entire house on a weekend. That's not possible!

I've learned to think, and say, "I'm going to dust my nativities and the shelves they're on this weekend." Or, "I'm going to choose clothes I'll never wear again to give away and see if I need to buy anything for the season." These accurate, realistic statements—the truth—have helped me be successful and encouraged.

Is this relevant to your children? Is your son thinking, "I'm going to write my paper tonight." That's overwhelming—so he might not even start. Or even if he gets a good start, he won't write the whole paper so he still may be discouraged at the end of the night. What he should have thought and told you was, "I'm going to research topics and settle on one tonight. I'll keep track of my sources and read two or three in more detail tomorrow night." These things, your son can achieve. He'll be less frustrated and more successful. More motivated!

Provide Evidence

Are there times when you doubt people's compliments and corrections? I know there are times I do. Unfortunately, children sometimes think you're lying when you're not. Have you noticed they may not believe you when your comments surprise them? If they think they're amazing, your correction won't register. If they think they can't do anything right, your compliment won't help. The key to both is to provide the evidence that supports your conclusion. This is what makes your compliments and corrections believable. Evidence will help your children grow and increase their motivation in the right direction.

You can use the camera on your phone to collect evidence of messy rooms, unfinished homework they were supposed to complete before playing games, and bad attitudes. You can also take pictures of your son's great accomplishment for proof in the future that he is more capable than he thinks he is. I'm not suggesting you spy on your children, but it's your right to use pictures and video to collect evidence if your children continually doubt you. It's a consequence of their choice to not believe your words.

Often your words will suffice. Your power phrase is "I know because . . . " For example, you might say, "You're being disorganized. *I know because* it takes you way too long to find everything you need to get out the door on time." Or, "You're being disrespectful. *I know because* you debate everything we say and question our decisions rather than responding obediently." Evidence doesn't lie.

We can use the same formula when affirming children. "You're musically talented. *I know because* you quickly learned a lot about playing the flute well." Or, "You're being compassionate. *I know because* when Lyla fell, you went to see if she was okay."

Being able to say "I know because . . ." means you've listened and watched carefully. This observational power is something you need to use. To do so, you'll need to be fully present often.

Say What You Mean and Mean What You Say

Picture your children asking you for something they'd like. Answer truthfully. Don't say "Maybe" or "We'll see" if the answer is "No." Don't give them false hope. If you do, when you later tell them "No," there will be greater disappointment and possibly more complaining than if you would have been honest initially.

If you need to discuss your children's question with your spouse, that's fine. But don't always make your spouse be the one who has to say "No." That's not fair. Be courageous. Say "No" to the no things and "Yes" to the yes things. Rarely say "Maybe." When you have to, explain what information you need to make a decision. For example, you may need to call the host of the party your children want to attend. Or you might need time to pray. You may need to ask your spouse about his or her schedule for the day in question. Let your children know and be sure to tell them when you will get back to them with the answer. You will build trust and positive relationships, both of which are essential to being able to motivate your children well.

Here's another example of how to use language carefully. One of the most consistent complaints I hear from children is that parents tell them to improve, but don't acknowledge it when they do. For instance, your son's science grades might be consistently in the 80s so you talk with him, encourage him, and ask him to improve. Within a few days, he shows you a graded paper with a 92% at the top. He wants to hear "Great, you did it! I knew you could." Or, "Way to improve! I'm proud of you." He did improve and that's what you said you wanted, but too often children tell me, "They didn't say 'good' or 'thank you.' They just said 'you can do better.'" Then they sometimes add, "If they wanted me to be perfect I wish they would have said that."

> Too many children conclude, "I can never please my parents."

If you ask your son to improve, acknowledge it when he does. Later, when the time is right, you could set the next goal for him or, better yet, ask him what he thinks he might score on the next assignment, quiz, or test. Allow space between your joy that improvement occurred and your discussion about the next goal. Otherwise, your son may interpret it in one of the most damaging ways of all. Too many children conclude, "I can never please my parents." If they think this, they may stop trying. It will now be unlikely that you'll have much motivational power.

If you recognize you've done some of the things I've recommended against here, you're not alone. It's okay. Your relationship and your kids' motivation can improve. You weren't intentionally setting out to damage or demotivate your children. Talk about this. Share some examples and apologize. Ask to be forgiven. If it's appropriate, and they've been doing the same thing, you could ask them if they'd like to use clearer and more honest language, too. If you do this, make sure they know you are still taking responsibility for your actions.

Use Words Carefully

"Have fun at school!"

How did your parents send you out the door to school? My mom said, "Put your thinking cap on" and "Think and listen." Maybe yours did, too.

A sure way for children to get the wrong idea about school (and Sunday school) is for a parent to say "Have fun today!"

Having fun is not the purpose of school. Planting the idea that school will be fun sets kids up to be disappointed. This expectation and lack of fulfillment messes with their motivation.

I want school to be enjoyable, but it doesn't need to be fun. Not everything can be fun; some elements of school are work. Plain and simple.

If after school you ask first, "Did you have fun today?" or "What did you do that was fun?" you're again giving your kids permission to be unhappy with school and their teachers. This will decrease their motivation.

Ask what they learned and enjoyed. Ask what surprised them and what made them curious. Ask if they helped someone and how it made them feel. Ask if they noticed someone was lonely and how they responded. Ask what they did that made them feel successful. Ask what they're motivated to learn more about. If they tell you they had fun, respond with joy. If they complain they didn't, coach them to understand that entire days of fun are probably not realistic. Help them understand teachers' goals and the complexity of teaching.

"Easy" and "hard"

Children might be motivated when you tell them a chore, task, or assignment will be easy. But others will be hesitant because you've told them this in the past and it wasn't true. If your daughter looks at an assignment or begins to do the assigned task and it's not easy, she can quickly feel dumb. Now she'll be less motivated. And she may not trust you the next time you say something is easy.

Telling children something is hard doesn't work all the time either. Some children are motivated by challenges. Others aren't. If children are insecure, haven't been successful lately, or don't want to disappoint you, they may now resist this task or assignment. They're demotivated.

Remember that evidence doesn't lie. If you know why something should be easy, let your son know. Do you have proof that he recently did well on a very similar task or assignment? Use specific language and examples from the past to help him relax and be motivated to embrace the task.

Respond with truth if your daughter looks at an assignment and declares, "This is going to be hard!" Remember, she needs to be able to trust you for your relationship to be solid. Don't flippantly respond, "You haven't even tried yet!" or "Why are you always so pessimistic?" Instead, coach and cheer. Tell her it's new, but that doesn't necessarily mean it will be hard. Remind her that the purpose of school is to learn new things. Teach her how the task is similar to tasks she's done well. Coach by telling her which of her strengths will come in handy. Remind her that she can ask you for specific help.

"You are being . . ." and "You are"

A sure way to discourage children is to react to a negative quality as if it's a permanent condition. Some conditions are permanent—I'm permanently tall and spelling will never be my strength. But when we know a child is going through a stage or had a rare negative day, we must be careful not to imply it's permanent.

This is why I like the power phrase "You are being . . ." rather than proclaiming, "*You are* irresponsible" which sounds like it's a permanent character quality the child can't change, you can say, "*You are being* irresponsible." This reminds you and the child that it was her choice in the moment to not do what she was told.

One more thing. Using "You are being" for positive qualities is just as wise as using it for negatives. You want your children to know that their strengths, healthy character, and honorable ways of doing their chores are all decisions you're proud of. Although these decisions and behaviors can become permanent or close to it (praise God!) especially when your children are first developing the strength, reminding them it's always their decision will motivate them and remind them of their personal responsibility.

"Earn" and "get"

An easy way to remind children that they're responsible for their choices and their outcomes is to use the word "earn" and not "get" especially when talking about grades. When asking about a test score or the grade on an assignment, ask "What grade did you *earn?*" not "What grade did you *get?*"

"Get" implies the grade was given to your children. "Earn" reminds them something they did or didn't do caused the grade. Moms who have heard me teach this are requiring their children to show them work and say, "Look Mom. I *earned* a 96%" instead of "Look Mom. I *got* a 96%." It hasn't taken long for the children to use the words right. This one change has helped children own their grades and argue less about them. Moms are reporting their children are more motivated.

When they earn a good grade, comment or ask about what they did that they can do again to earn similar results. When they earn a lower grade, ask what they could do differently to improve their learning and their grade when they do something similar. Do not allow them to give their negative grade away by blaming teachers, you, the weather, or anything else. They *earned* it.

"Want" and "need"

The use of "want" and "need" is another example of how accurate language can make a positive difference as you parent to get children on your side, to believe you, and to do what you ask. If you "need" your son to empty the dishwasher, don't tell him you "want" him to. If you "need" your daughter to feed the dog, don't tell her you "want" her to. They may not verbalize their internal thought, but it may be, "Well, I don't want to."

How do you use these words? I can be guilty of saying, "I *need* onion rings with my burger." No, I don't. I *want* them. Or, "I *want* to go to the gym." That should have been, "I *need* to go to the gym." Listen to yourself, especially when talking with your children. The correct use of these words can decrease frustration and increase trust, cooperation, and motivation.

Maybe how these two words come up with technology is the perfect teachable moment you can use. Parents often ask me, "When should I get my child a phone?" My response is always "When they *need* a phone." If your children whine and try to manipulate you into giving them want they want, use the teachable moment. Talk with your kids about the difference between wanting something and needing something.

Many parents have lost the courage to say "no" when their kids ask for technology. I understand. Just because children want something should not mean that they get it. If you give in with technology, your children will believe they can get you to say "yes" to other things as well. (My book, *Screens and Teens: Connecting with Our Kids in a Wireless World* will help you understand why technology is such a draw and how to handle issues like this.)

Parent strong and be brave. Use "need" and "want" appropriately and expect your kids to as well.

Use Consistent Comebacks
When They Complain

One of the best ways to beat the complaining monster is to use consistent comebacks when children whine and complain. Your words will teach children they can't manipulate you. They'll learn to ask for help rather than just complain.

I became especially convinced of the power of consistent comebacks for consistent complaints when I learned to golf. Nancy, my friend and teacher, made it clear from the very beginning that I wasn't allowed to say, "I can't." At first I complained because the game was more complicated than I realized. But Nancy explained that she knew I'd need ongoing coaching, but she didn't want me to defeat myself by saying, "I can't."

By not allowing me to say this, Nancy empowered me to ask for specific help. This meant I had to think about why I was confused. If I asked, "How do I position my front foot again?" she was willing to answer me. If I asked about my follow-through, she answered me. She just wanted me to identify where I was confused and learn to ask for help. She knew what I also knew. Hearing myself say "I can't" wasn't going to do me any good. It's not motivational.

When your children complain, stop entering into long discussions that distract you and allow children to waste time. Too often complaints become arguments and power struggles ensue. Rather, use consistent, brief responses regularly. (Are you old enough to understand the broken record analogy? Say the same thing over and over again.) You'll be teaching your children they can't manipulate you or get you to change expectations. That's part of the power of the method. It will increase children's motivation in the right direction.

> Too often complaints become arguments and power struggles ensue.

This is a bit tricky because you need to be available to your children. Earlier, I wrote that you must listen longer. Your children do need to be heard. It's essential to having a healthy relationship. But sometimes an appropriate consequence for not listening to you and for questioning your authority is that you don't engage in conversation. Not arguing will enhance your relationship.

"I can't!" and "This is too hard!"

For example, when a child declares, "I can't," when you introduce a problem or chore, a great comeback is: "What *can* you do?" I've had children tell me they can't do it and after I ask them what they can do, they start rattling off, "Well, I could do . . ." Before they know it, they are admitting to me that they can do it! It can be pretty funny.

"I can't" was their cop-out rooted in insecurity. "I can't" was protecting them from possible failure. "I can't" invited you to rescue them by doing some of their work for them. Their "I can't" was a habit from past interactions with people they didn't trust. Talk about these roots when you identify them. You may also want to talk about how much we can learn from mistakes, that you value risk-taking, and that your grace and God's is available.

When you ask, "What can you do?" you might get a response like this, "Well, I could do it if it was a double-digit instead of a triple-digit number." Then let them do some double-digit problems, watch them, and encourage them. Then, after success, encourage them to add the third digit.

Another comeback that works for "I can't" and also when they declare, "This is too hard!" is to ask, "*How* can I help?" Don't ask, "Can I help?" because they can say "No." Instead, declare your availability by using the word "How?"

If they whine back at you, "This is too hard!" repeat, "*How* can I help?" Continue the persistence that you're there for them. Train them to ask you for specific help. Sometimes they just need a ruler, but they love that complaining gives them power over you. "*How* can I help?" takes away a lot of the negative power.

Sometimes "What don't you understand?" also works well. This implies that it's okay to have questions or to be confused.

You're giving them permission to ask clarifying questions. Maybe they need more instruction. Maybe they need to be coached.

I also like the comeback, "You can trust me." Again, if you're confident that the task or assignment is appropriate, your children need to learn to trust you. You will not ask them to do something they can't do. This doesn't mean it will all be easy, but it does mean success is possible.

Would you like another comeback for "This is hard!"? If you've earned the right, respond with something like, "It's all good." That's what my trainer, Linda, often does in the gym. If I want her to know that I'm aware she made something more challenging by adding weight or reps, she smiles, moves toward the next apparatus, and declares, "It's all good." It's her way of reminding me I can trust her to plan a workout that's appropriately challenging so I'll grow. And isn't that what you want for children? I tell them often that if everything were easy, it wouldn't be good for them. Learning and helping around the house with new chores and responsibilities are all a part of maturing.

"I don't want to!"

My favorite comeback when kids boldly announce that they don't want to do what they're told is, "Because . . . ?" When you use a tone of voice inviting an answer, they'll learn to provide the details. "I don't want to because I was going to text Stephanie to ask a question about our concert." Or, "I don't want to because I need to change before I cut the lawn."

Wouldn't it be great if these children wouldn't even say "I don't want to," but just ask you, "May I text Stephanie first?" and "May I change my clothes first?" Some don't because they love the power they get from frustrating you. Too many don't think they have permission to ask things like this. Possibly, when they tried to ask for a delay in the past, you didn't fully listen and assumed they were totally trying to get out of work.

I also encourage you to respond with "Already answered" or "Not negotiable." Just keep saying it, possibly walking toward them if the first few repetitions don't work. If you believe you're asking them to do something they're capable of doing, then don't let them manipulate you into changing your mind. Be brave and parent strong.

"This isn't fun!"

Maybe your son complains when beginning chores or assignments, "This isn't fun." What could your comeback be? You could ignore him. You could respond, "I know. That's not the point. Do it anyway." Or, "The sooner you do it, the more time you'll have for fun." You can also acknowledge his feelings by saying, "I'm sorry you don't think so."

Experiment and find the one or two statements that work.

If he keeps repeating, "It's not fun!" you can repeat, "Do it anyway."

"I'm stupid!"

One of the best comebacks for "I'm stupid!" is "Prove it." As I wrote earlier, they can't prove they're stupid. They can prove they forgot there was a quiz, chose to be lazy, tripped over something, or the like. Have them reword this statement as truth.

Depending on the situation and how often you hear "I'm stupid!" it's also appropriate to let them know you're sad for them because you know feeling stupid doesn't feel good. You could simply say, "I'm sorry." Then ask, "Would you like to tell me what happened?" Based on their answer, you can redirect them to see the truth.

WHEN THEY SAY	SAY ONE OF THESE:
"I CAN'T!"	"What can you do?" "How can I help?" "What don't you understand?" "You can trust me." "You can when you try." "You can when you . . ."

"THIS IS TOO HARD!"	"How can I help?" "What don't you understand?" "You can trust me." "It's all good."
"I DON'T WANT TO."	"Because . . ." "Not negotiable." "Already answered."
"THIS ISN'T FUN!"	"I know. That's not the point. Do it anyway." "I'm sorry you don't think so." "The sooner you do it, the more time you'll have for fun." "Not negotiable."
"I'M STUPID!" "THIS IS STUPID!"	"Prove it!" "I'm sad you feel this way." "Would you like to tell me what happened?"

WHAT ABOUT YOU?

Think back to your childhood, teen years, and life as a young adult. In what ways do you think you'd be different if your parents would have listened to you longer and better? Or, if they did a great job at that, how do you know it positively affected you? Also, think about whether you're believing any lies about yourself. Are any inconsistencies in your life possibly due to some lies? Pray and possibly talk with those you trust.

THINGS TO DO

- Accurate and effective communication really is a major key in motivation. Which of the suggestions from this chapter will you use first? Which will benefit you and your children the most? Providing evidence? Correcting lies? Using "want" and "need" accurately? Listening longer? One of the other ideas? I hope you'll make a choice and put one idea into practice. Then, when it becomes more natural, come back to the chapter to choose the next idea to implement. If your children notice your changes, let them know what you're doing and why. These discussions can be very beneficial.

- What do you think of the consistent comeback idea? Do your kids use some of the statements I address? Which comeback might you start with? Don't give up if it doesn't feel natural at first. Be consistent— that's part of the power of the comebacks. Does one or more children use a different complaint that you can come up with a comeback for? Make a plan and

• follow through. Practice repeating the comebacks. Parent strong and long. You can do this.

THINGS TO THINK ABOUT

• What's something you've been trying to motivate one or more children to do? How could you increase their motivation by providing evidence of your concern?

• Have you gotten into the habit of lying to yourself about yourself? Of allowing your children to lie to themselves about themselves? What conversation might you have first?

• How does the phrase "You are being" apply to your children? Could you start using it in hopes of increasing their personal responsibility for a character quality or two? Which kids and which qualities?

Listen to advice and accept instruction, that
you may gain wisdom in the future.

PROVERBS 19:20

Complimenting and Correcting

I often say that the words we speak and the words we don't speak change lives. Scripture tells us words can bring life or death (Proverbs 18:21), and they can set on fire the entire course of a life (James 3:5–6). They also reveal what's really in our hearts (Matthew 12:33–35).

Words you use to compliment and correct children can either guide them in the right direction or take the wind out of their sails. They wield great power and value when they're used well. Compliments can encourage children to keep doing well or cause them to develop unhealthy pride. Corrections can inspire children to positive action or wound them. Paralysis of all kinds is possible. Children may choose not to risk again and to create distance between themselves and you.

Part of the power of offering feedback well is that you can help children meet their core needs in healthy ways. Correcting and complimenting well is essential to building security and creating healthy relationships within the family and beyond. Because children also learn much about their identity from compliments and corrections, this core need is affected, too. As you remember from chapter 4, these first three needs definitely influence children's purpose and competence. And, of course, since competence is dependent upon doing things well, complimenting to affirm strengths and correcting to change weaknesses are significant ways this core need can be met.

There's both a skill and a will to providing feedback in healthy and helpful ways. We need knowledge and a heart to encourage and instruct. You've already read much in this book that will help you use compliments and corrections effectively. I'm looking forward to you understanding some nuances about these powerful words that will pay great dividends. Feedback can direct children's motives, redirect them toward goals you want them to value, encourage them when they lack courage, help them stop negative behaviors, motivate them to continue making wise choices, and so much more.

Definitions and Differences

If you have heard me speak, you probably know I enjoy words. One of my strongest intelligences is word smart. I enjoy looking up definitions of words even when I already think I know them. I'm rarely disappointed. That has certainly been the case with the important words in this chapter. Let's take a look at some of the words and ideas behind feedback.[1]

Flattery

Flattery doesn't help anyone, but I hear people use it far too often. It's like fingernails on a chalkboard to me. If you're too young to know what I mean, think about the most obnoxious ringtone that won't stop. Maybe that is today's equivalent.

Flattery is used to "try to please someone by complimentary remarks or attention." It's "insincere, excessive, or exaggerated praise" that's used to manipulate the person, often so the one using it gains favor and gets something. They do it to build themselves up rather than to encourage the one they're praising. Flattery definitely can wound and confuse people. Sadly, I can be guilty of using it. When I realize I am, I always evaluate which core need isn't being met well. That's always the issue.

If you use it with children, they'll learn not to trust you. If you use flattery, rather than a compliment, you won't be building them up. They'll figure out you're trying to build up yourself. Rather than being motivated, they may become defeated.

Compliments

Complimenting is appropriate. A compliment is "an expression of praise, commendation, or admiration." Commendation and recommendation are related. When you commend with words of support, you recommend these people to others. So not only does the person you're complimenting benefit personally, but relationally as well.

When I looked up the definition of "compliment," I was

delighted with a small surprise. An archaic definition is "a gift or present." I love that! Many times, someone cares enough to compliment me and it feels like a gift. Have you experienced that, too? It was exactly what I needed to hear to give me the energy to keep writing or doing whatever was relevant to the affirmation. A compliment can surprise your children and provide a similar lift as a physical gift designed to encourage.

Note the differences between compliments and flattery. Then ask yourself which you most often do.

COMPLIMENT	FLATTERY
Sincere praise, admiration, commendation	Insincere praise
Truly deserved; based on something real	Not deserved; may praise something unimportant or that didn't actually happen
Affirm to encourage children	Affirm to manipulate children
Build up children receiving compliment	Build up self in the eyes of children being praised

Criticism

Criticism is defined as "passing severe judgment; censure; faultfinding." My favorite definition is found in my *New Shorter Oxford English Dictionary*—"to point out an error." Both these definitions make it clear that criticisms aren't helpful. Passing judgment, finding fault, and pointing out errors do not help children change. It's true that children need to know what to change out of, but it can't be the only thing they know. Criticisms don't encourage. They don't motivate. They can serve to cement children's identity with the very negatives you'd like to change.

I imagine I can safely predict that you don't want to be critical. But are you sometimes? Sure. We all are. It's something we have to fight against. Hopefully, if you criticize at all, it's because you're tired, not feeling well, unusually frustrated, or distracted. Hopefully you haven't *chosen* to be critical and criticizing is not want you *want* to do.

If you criticize more often than you'd like, it might be a habit and it may be due to what you heard growing up. Maybe you're negative, looking for perfection, or discouraged. Those are all reasons, but not excuses to continue. Earlier chapters and the instruction here may be just what you need to break through the negativity and reverse the habit.

I'll never forget hearing a principal shout to a student, "I don't want any more of that attitude!" The boy quickly looked at me and said, "I'm in really big trouble. That's the only attitude I have."

Corrections

Children need to be corrected because they're learning and, like us all, they're imperfect and they make mistakes, unwise choices, and unfortunate decisions. Parents should be a source of important, life-changing corrections. A correction "sets or makes true, accurate, or right; removes the errors or faults from." Improvement, not judgment, is the goal. The *New Shorter Oxford English Dictionary* defines correction as "to put right an error." Do you see how different that is from the definition of criticism—"point out an error"?

> **Parents should be a source of important, life-changing corrections.**

If all you do is tell children what they're doing wrong, you're criticizing. When you include information that will help them change, you're correcting. That's a powerful difference. Correcting requires careful observation and for you to use more words. It may also require an attitude change on your part. You must be interested in helping children improve rather than just pointing out what's wrong and maybe getting some perverse power from putting them in their place.

Note how correction and criticism are different. Which do you most often use when trying to motivate your children?

CORRECTION	CRITICISM
Sets or makes true, accurate, or right; removes the errors or faults from	Passing severe judgment; censure; faultfinding
To put right an error	To point out an error
Used to help children improve; used well, correction can build children up	Used to judge children; often used to control and put down
Must include instruction	Does not include instruction
There is such a thing as helpful correction	There is no such thing as constructive criticism

Purposes of Compliments and Corrections

Understanding why complimenting and correcting are powerful communication and motivational tools will further help you use them well. Exactly what can your words do?

Compliments teach children what to repeat

Compliments teach children what to repeat. In this way, they affect the future and don't just judge the past. By telling children what you like, you can get more of it—beliefs, attitudes, actions, decisions, character traits, emotions, and more. This will especially occur when we're specific, which I write about at the end of this chapter.

Don't compliment to get more of children's good behavior so your life is easier. Compliment because it's good for your children and affects their character. Success breeds success, and you're creating this opportunity when you affirm them. (Of course, a side benefit is that your life will be easier. Just don't compliment for that reason only.)

Exclamations like "Fabulous!" and "That's wonderful!" can encourage children. Offering praise ("expressing approval") and being a cheerleader, as I addressed in chapter 6, are often appropriate. Just remember that simply being told something is "fabulous" doesn't guarantee children can repeat what they just did. I've had more children than I can count turn to me and say, "I wish I knew what she liked so I could do it again." Specific compliments have teaching power.

Consider including "I'm glad because . . ." statements with your compliments. Especially if they respect you, these can motivate children to do the same thing again, therefore affecting the future. Don't overdo this. Gradually withdraw these statements so your children develop more intrinsic motivation. You don't want them doing what they're doing just because of your emotional response. It can jumpstart them, but they do need to discover intrinsic reasons for maintaining healthy behavior. Asking them if their behavior has made them glad can be a good transition.

Many parents have found this order of phrases helpful:

"You showed great *initiative*. Remember, we talked about that word? *I know you used* initiative because you got started with your homework while I was helping Seth instead of relying on me. *I'm glad because* you're growing in obedience and understanding that time is valuable. You also honored your brother and me by being willing to be independent. Thank you."

Corrections teach children what not to repeat

By pointing out what's wrong *and* offering reliable help so children can change, specific corrections can teach them what *not* to repeat. When we correct well, we'll get less of what is unhealthy and undesirable. Corrections should affect the future and not just judge the past. Using "I'm *not* glad because . . ." statements with your corrections can work well just as "I'm glad because . . ." statements work with compliments.

Don't correct your children because you like the power. Correct them because you know they'll be better off with right choices and behaviors. It should always be about them and their heart. Corrections, not criticisms, have the power to redirect children's beliefs, motivation, and behavior. Children will believe they can change habits because you're not just telling them what's wrong. Your words are also teaching them what to do instead.

When you are frustrated with your son, remember your words should affect his future and help him know what *not* to repeat. Think more about what you want him to do next time than the way he just did it. This will change your tone of voice and the words you use. He'll be changed, too, and not just feel judged.

> "You were *not careful*. You were being *careless*. *I know because* you didn't look to see what else was on the table before you tossed your backpack up there. We've talked about this before. *I'm not glad* you partially crushed the strawberries *because* you told us earlier in the week that you would work to remember to be careful. We need you to honor your word. What do you think?"

Because corrections must include instruction, use a "Therefore statement" after you point out what's wrong or disappointing. You won't always use the word "therefore," but instruction is necessary to make sure you're not criticizing children. That's what the question, "What do you think?" is designed to elicit in the above example. This can work well when children are old enough and you have talked with them about the issue enough. You'll interact with your son about his ideas, resulting in helpful examples and instruction.

Using the word "therefore" or something similar causes us to add instruction and hope. We don't leave children thinking about what they've done. We leave them thinking about what they can do.

Picture this conversation you might have with your young child: "I can tell you're scared that your friends might break your favorite toys and that's why you're yelling at them. That's not the way we treat others and we'll talk more about that later. Therefore, before you have friends over to play next time, I'll help you put away the toys you don't want to play with that day so you won't be nervous. From then on, I'll expect you to remember to do this on your own. Is this a good idea?"

Here's another example: "You're being a poor sport. I know because you've been pouting and quiet ever since you lost the game to your sister. I'm not glad because we are a family unit, and you know we want you to support each other. You are stealing her joy. I'm also concerned that your behavior might be rooted in pride. We've talked with you about the reality that you can't always win and you don't know everything yet. Therefore, I found this book about sports heroes who had to work hard to develop their skills. They lost a lot of games on the way to winning. Reading it together will be fun and give us lots to talk about. What do you think about your attitude toward your sister? May I help you apologize or are you ready to on your own? Also, until your mom and I think you can play with her without hurting her if she wins, we will not allow you to play games like this one. What do you think?"

It's rare that I speak on this topic and don't have many parents admit to me that they've been criticizing and not correcting their children. It wasn't their intent; I doubt it's yours. Remember that your power is the "Therefore . . ." statement. It causes you to coach. Or, you can teach more if that's what they need.

The following statements are all criticisms because the mom has only pointed out what is wrong. Picture yourself turning these into corrections by adding instruction. Be careful! "Try again" and "do it over" and "you should know better" are not instructive statements. They just add judgment and then fear if children honestly don't know how to please you.

"Your bedroom is not clean."

"You call that finished?"

"You're leaving that towel there?"

"I don't like the way you treated your sister."

"I'm disappointed that you earned a B- on your English paper."

Emphasize things children control

Correcting and complimenting things children control is another way you affect their future. You want them to take appropriate credit for their successes. It's not about pride. Rather, this is essential for them to be able to repeat what they've done well. You can't allow them to believe success was due to luck, your mood, easy questions, or other things outside their control. If they do, they won't believe they can be successful again. This will decrease motivation.

Rather, if you overhear your son say, "I was lucky! The questions were easy!" you can respond with something like, "You weren't lucky. You told me you were listening better in class. The other night, you asked me for help when you were confused. I saw you studying instead of gaming. I think the questions were easy because you studied the right material enough. You made smart decisions."

The same thing is true when children appear to give away responsibility for their mistakes. Do you know children who believe their grades were due to the teacher's bad mood, unfair questions, or the fact you made them babysit their younger sister so they didn't have time to study? When you are partly responsible, you need to own that and apologize. You can also empower children to tell you if your plans or requests don't work well for them. You can help children understand that questions seemed unfair because they didn't study as much as they could have. And if they knew they were going to babysit the night before the test, you can talk with them about time management. These conversations allow children to change and grow.

As you discuss their successes, help them decide whether to use the same strategies again. If it helped when they looked up words at www.thesaurus.com, to get a complete understanding of the words, maybe they should do that more often. Did it help them to rewrite their notes or didn't it? Did it help to read the text out loud?

You can do the same thing when talking about their completion of tasks. Why did they efficiently clean their bathroom one day and not another? What's different on the days you don't have to remind them to put their toys away? Help them determine why they're successful and what to do again or never again.

You could make a list with your children of things they control. This could be very revealing, as they may list things they actually don't control and not list things they do. They control how much they practice. They control whether they study and how much. They control their efforts, perseverance, teachability, other character qualities, and their own motivation. They decide whether to ask for help, use Scripture, pray, go to sleep when they're tired, and more. This activity and talking about control will increase their personal responsibility.

Increase hope by providing feedback about ability
  and character

Children find hope for today and tomorrow when they understand their successes and challenges are always due to a combination of how they are competent *and* how they apply themselves. Believing it's one or the other can lead to perfectionism, procrastination, laziness, and fear. Therefore, it's important to compliment and correct the character qualities *and* other things children use that contribute to their successes. This can include their study strategies, the way they are smart, and their genius qualities. (I'll address these in the next chapter.)

Evidence is clear. Parents who cause children to think their successes are due only to their intelligence, and don't also talk about the role of character, create a dangerous situation.[2] Now, if their children don't do well, they can only blame their lack of intelligence. This can quickly result in hopelessness and lowered expectations because they don't think they have any control over that.

Carol Dweck's work on these ideas is convincing.[3] She has consistently found that children praised for using effort tackled more challenging tasks than those praised just for ability or for the quality of their work. This is partly due to these compliments causing a release of dopamine in the brain. The "feel-good" effect encourages children to hang in there. When

affirmed for using initiative, effort, diligence, and perseverance, children learn these are admirable qualities and they're
wise to use them. They're not necessary because of a lack of
ability. They're necessary because not all learning is easy—nor
should it be! When being complimented for using them, children learn to persevere in spite of obstacles, and they develop
resiliency. Mistakes don't scare them. They learn they can either study to increase ability or use more effort next time.

This is a great opportunity to teach resilience. As I addressed in chapter 1, learning to be resilient is important. It
allows children to bounce back quickly from defeat, stress, and
trauma. Resilient children will overcome adversity and not be
defined by it. They know failure isn't fatal or final. It's a normal
part of growth and life. They learn they must get up and try
again.[4] I imagine this is what you want for your children.

Develop their entire identity

Your compliments and corrections teach children who they
are. This matters greatly because identity controls behavior.
Who we think we are is who we will be. If children's identity
is narrow because you only talk with them about one part,
they'll struggle especially when that part fails them. Work to
prioritize complimenting and correcting their decisions, behaviors, and attitudes for all six components.[5]

One component is their character, which I addressed in

chapter 2. (Remember Appendix A is a list of character qualities.) The other components are the intellectual self, emotional
self, social self, physical self, and spiritual self.[6] Complimenting and correcting attributes of each is a powerful way to help
children mature.

A few summers ago, I was privileged to spend one week
teaching four hundred seventh graders about their five core
needs. We talked about the importance of developing a broad,
healthy identity. In small groups, they listed what they would
want their identity to be for each of the six components. I've
listed their answers in Appendix D. You'll be encouraged. Perhaps this would be a valuable exercise to do with your children.

Improve self-evaluation

In many aspects of parenting, thinking about working your
way out of a job might be appropriate. Don't get me wrong.
I know you'll be a parent forever, and you'll hopefully have a
delightful friendship with adult children who will want your
ideas and input. And you'll want theirs. However, like others I
know, do you dream of the day when your children will need
you less?

For children to move toward appropriate independence and keep maturing, they need help learning to evaluate themselves realistically. This is your job as a parent from
the day they're born—to teach and train them for healthy

independence while they still want to be a vibrant part of your family. It must be a goal of the feedback you provide. It's a very valuable way you can affect their future.

When you're able, explaining the "why" behind your comments can improve success and motivation. Why were you satisfied with the way your son straightened his room today and you weren't a few days ago? As you drove home from youth group, frustrated with your daughter's attitude, does she know why?

Technology is partly to blame for children's inability or unwillingness to evaluate themselves.[7] Children who play games/apps are used to the scoring being done for them instantly and objectively. They don't have to think about how they're doing. The device will tell them.

Children are used to earning higher and higher scores and winning often. That's how the designers keep them addicted (possibly) and playing. Scoring is very positive. Your children may have a hard time evaluating themselves negatively even when it's well deserved.

Believing the world revolves around them and they must remain special is another reason correcting themselves and taking responsibility for things that go wrong can be so difficult. They may be better at identifying strengths, and possibly exaggerating them, than they are at owning their weaknesses.

Technology has taught children that everything should be

easy. Therefore, it's hard for them to admit they had to persevere and yet still made mistakes.

Sometimes have children tell you how they think they did
before you offer your opinions. If they're relatively accurate,
affirm them specifically. When they're not, have the conversation. If you think their inability to see errors or their need to
puff themselves up is related to technology, point that out.
Possibly decrease their tech time.

If it was a character issue, use specific language so they can
believe you. For example, maybe your daughter didn't thor-
oughly clean up everything from the project she completed.
She might say she hurried because she wanted to play with
a friend. Maybe you saw it as laziness or disrespect. Remember—words are very powerful. Use the right ones.

How might your children internalize self-evaluation? How
can it become a natural part of who they are? For some kids,
a journal is an effective self-evaluation tool. They can keep it
private or show it to you so you can discuss what they're dealing with. Pay attention to see if they're learning to evaluate
all components of their identity. Help your children find out
what self-evaluation method works best for them.

Attributes of Effective Feedback

Choosing to be optimistic, positive, encouraging, and enthusiastic will be essential to your ability to consistently provide

excellent feedback. Remembering to coach, cheer, and referee with compliments and corrections will help children. Working to provide feedback that can be described with the following attributes will serve you and your children well.

Specific and believable

Telling children they've done a "good job" may be encouraging, but the encouragement won't last because they won't know what to do to repeat the "good job." Fear can set in because they're not sure they can please you again.

What made something good? Tell them that. Was it complete, accurate, unique, thoughtfully done, or imaginative? What made your child good? Was he or she confident, patient, sincere, industrious, or focused? What displeased you? Was your son prideful, careless, or self-centered? Was your daughter demanding or sarcastic? Specific words like these communicate to your children that you have watched and listened. Your investment helps them pay more attention to what you say. You are more believable. This builds security. And, of course, it builds success. To help you move from general to specific, I've listed many complimenting words in Appendix E and correcting words in Appendix F.

To make your compliments and corrections even more believable, provide the evidence for your feedback as you read about in chapter 7. Especially when your children don't think

COMPLIMENTING AND CORRECTING 225

well of themselves, they'll doubt compliments. If they think they do everything right, they'll doubt corrections. Evidence doesn't lie. Do you remember your power phrase? "I know because . . ." (As I often teach, don't do this all the time. It will get tiresome for you and your children. Anything well done, overdone, is badly done.)

Do you remember that the purpose of compliments is to get more of the good? That's why you must be specific. For example, when I'm presenting at a conference, I value eye contact from individuals in my audience. It helps me connect with them. From looking into their eyes and at their faces, I've learned to tell if they're confused or curious, being thoughtful or getting bored, and eager to learn more or overwhelmed by what I already taught.

Therefore, I look for an opportunity to compliment my audiences about their eye contact. It's almost always a fun experience. I say something like, "Thanks for the eye contact. It helps me gain energy from you, and I can tell by looking at your faces if you're confused, frustrated, or curious. So, thanks for the eye contact."

As soon as I start saying this, heads pop up and everyone looks at me. They don't wait until I'm finished. No. As soon as I say "eye contact," they look up. They laugh and admit they wish I was looking in their direction. They want to do what I want them to do. They respect me and want to do what's helpful. From now until the end of my presentation, every time our eyes meet they will feel good about themselves even if I never mention it again. Specific compliments motivate children to stay motivated in the right direction doing the right thing.

Specific compliments and corrections are *memorable*. They make it much easier for children to repeat the positive things and not repeat the negative things. One statement lasts a long time when it's specific and believable. Providing the reason for wanting a behavior to continue (as I did with my eye contact statement) or not continue can further empower children.

Helpful and thoughtful

There's absolutely a place for cheerleader compliments. Dr. Anthony Gregorc's fascinating work about Mind Styles™ is relevant here.[8] He found that some people are satisfied to be told they did a "good" job. Words of higher praise put pressure on them they don't want. Others prefer being told they did "excellent" work. Others prefer the words "great, super, fantastic," or "superior." Watch your children when using these words and discern which they react well to.

- "Great job! I knew you could do it!"
- "Fantastic! That's so beautiful!"
- "That is excellent! I never would have been able to do that at your age."

There are times when short statements pointing out children's negative choices might also be enough. Maybe peers or siblings are present so you don't want to go into lots of details. Maybe you have corrected your children recently. Maybe you just want to remind them of what you know they know. (Don't do this often. You don't want to be critical. Your children won't approach you or trust you as often. And you won't be helping them nearly as much as a full correction.)

"You know better than that."

"I was disappointed in your attitude toward your grandmother. We just talked about this."

"You're not going to do what it looks like you're going to do, are you?"

Usually, however, you'll want your compliments and corrections to have more motivational power. That means they need to be more constructive. Remember, if you point out something wrong without offering a "therefore . . ." type statement, it's a criticism.

When you notice your son doing something wrong, if he or others are unsafe, speak up. "Stop!" "Put that down!!" When there are no emotional or physical safety issues due to what he is doing, wait before you speak. Observe longer. Listen more intently. Ideally you don't point out the trouble that concerns you until you can offer children hope they can change. Observing, and perhaps keeping a written record of the occurrences of the problem, can reveal solutions to talk about.

Is your son only bossy with a young neighbor boy?

Does your daughter become clingy and complaining only when she is hungry?

Is your son only critical toward himself and others after gaming?

Being a thoughtful and helpful parent as you compliment and correct your children will further establish their security in you. Let's discover six attributes of feedback that is thoughtful and helpful:

Know who they are

When you know your children well, you'll know if a task or assignment was easy or hard. If it was easy, and you over-compliment, they can feel dumb. (Your son thinks, "Did my dad actually think I couldn't do that? He must think I'm pretty stupid.") If something is quite challenging, and you criticize or offer too much correction, children can feel dumb and angry. ("I wish my mom understood how hard I studied and tried. No one did well. I can't ever please her.") If you think about it, I bet you've experienced how frustrating one or both of these situations can be. When you compliment and correct with knowledge about who your children are, they'll feel loved and safe with you. They'll want to listen to you.

Know their goals

Knowing your children's goals makes it easier to be thoughtful. If your daughter tells you she wants to improve her memorization of multiplication facts so she can do her work more quickly and accurately, ask about that when reviewing her papers and quizzes. She'll feel heard and supported. If your son wants to write with more adjectives and active verbs so you enjoy his stories more, talk about his word choice first when reviewing his story with him. He'll be more open to your input because you know it's something he wants to improve. Did all your children commit to not giving up quickly? Ask about that when talking about their school days.

Know your goals

Being thoughtful also means you remember your goals for your children. Maybe your oldest son prefers routine and likes to know in advance what his day will be like. That's his style and totally legitimate, but at the same time you need him to respect that plans sometimes must change. If you've talked with him about this, then you must look for opportunities to correct him and compliment him. It's not fair to bring up a concern and then not provide timely feedback. Especially when children are learning something new (an attitude, a behavior, or how to do a task) regular feedback is essential. For example:

"You were flexible. I know because you didn't complain when I ran errands in a different order than you expected. This made it easier for James. Thanks for understanding."

"You questioned me less about my need to change today's plans. I'm grateful you trusted me and you understand that you can't always have things the way you prefer. You made it less stressful for me. Thank you."

"What do you think was different about today? Did you recognize why you couldn't go with the flow as well as you have been? I have some thoughts and words that might describe some attitudes but think about it first and then I need you to share with me. I think you know what was going on. It wasn't accidental behavior."

Be fully present

Are your children fully present and able to listen and learn? Are you? If not, wait. Put down the technology, turn around so they can't be distracted by the traffic on the road, stop reading, be quiet for a bit, and then talk. If there still are many emotions being felt, wait longer. If you haven't collected your thoughts, wait longer.

Time it well

Sometimes the timing of your input can make or break the conversation. Did they just finish a stressful assignment or talk to a friend and you know the conversation didn't go well? Don't bring up a concern you have. It will feel to their heart like you're pouring salt on a wound. On the other hand, if your daughter just told you about her fabulous day, don't immediately tell her you're unhappy with how messy her bedroom is. She'll feel dismissed. She may believe you don't care about any of her victories, but only her struggles. Wait.

Pay attention to who's there

Paying attention to who's within earshot is another aspect of timing. It's not thoughtful or respectful to correct children in front of their peers or siblings. Doing it in front of adults is rarely helpful, too. (I don't need to add "criticize" to that sentence, right? Have you been convinced that isn't respectful or motivational?) Complimenting children in front of others can backfire, too. You can cause jealousy, bullying, competition, and probably other reactions you don't want to cause. Sometimes the complimented children will start doing worse because they didn't like getting teased for being the best. Sometimes those not complimented decide not to bother trying . . . "I can't be as good/smart as her."

Don't think of this as a "rule" you can never break.

Sometimes, affirming your son in front of his grandfather is totally appropriate. Perhaps his current view of his grandson is negative and critical for some reason. Maybe your daughter thinks her brother can't do anything right. Maybe you need to point out something he's done well recently to help her correct her lie. Have this conversation.

WHAT ABOUT YOU?

How are you doing? I realize I included a lot in this chapter. I truly don't want you overwhelmed. I hope you're identifying ideas most relevant to situations that caused you to read this book in the first place. Use those first and watch for positive reactions. Pray they'll become a natural part of your conversations and parenting. Then add new ideas. Don't do too much at once. Remember, too much of a good thing often isn't.

THINGS TO DO

- Look at the complimenting words on pages 265–67. Choose a few you want to strategically use for each of your children in the next week or two. Then choose a few new ones to prioritize for the next two weeks. This will help you see the positive behaviors and, as you use the words, your children will want to repeat these behaviors. Remember, we compliment to get more of the good we want.

- Look at the correcting words on pages 269–71. Are there some you can prioritize over the next week or two for each child? Have you been criticizing and you want to correct instead? Choosing the words in advance related to children's bad habits will increase your success.

THINGS TO THINK ABOUT

- If you believe you will make major changes to the way you compliment and correct your children, will it be smart to tell your children what you're doing and why? Why or why not? What will you do? When?

- Is criticism something you're in the habit of using? How will you make the change to correcting your children instead? What do you need to remember? How will you?

- Think of each of your children specifically. In what ways can your corrections and compliments become more thoughtful?

Whoever ignores instruction despises himself,
but he who listens to reproof gains
intelligence.

PROVERBS 15:32

You *Can* Help Your Child Learn

Why would I include a chapter about learning in a book about motivation? Because sometimes children want to do well on their academics, but they don't know how. All the stickers, bribes, and threats in the world won't help children engage with schoolwork and earn better grades if they need to be taught and coached. Is it possible that your children will be more motivated if you make some small adjustments in your approach and teach them some things about how they learn? Yes!

What you learn here will help you add variety to the methods you and your children use. Novelty is a proven motivator and using options gets the brain's attention.[1] And as you consider how your children learn best, assignments will be more meaningful and enjoyable. Your children will be more successful.

Environmental Preferences: How Do Children Best Concentrate?

Making changes in your children's environment can increase their ability to concentrate.[2] Therefore, they'll be more motivated. Knowing your children's preferences will help them and you. For example, if learning math is a struggle, you don't want them doing it when concentrating is also a challenge. You can observe them and ask them when they concentrate best. Empower them to make adjustments:

Time of day—Does your child prefer morning, afternoon, or evening?

Temperature—Does your child prefer a cold, cool, warm, or toasty environment?

Light—Does your child prefer bright fluorescent or incandescent light, dim light, or natural light?

Sound—Does your child concentrate best with silence, light background noise, or a noisy environment?

Mobility—Does your child do best when having the freedom to move during learning or is being motionless better?

Eating/drinking—Does your child concentrate best when eating and/or drinking or when not?

Seating—Does your child prefer a formal environment (e.g., desks and chairs) or informal (e.g., lying on the floor or bed)?

Alone or with others—Does your child concentrate best alone or when working with someone?

Modalities: How Do Children Best Remember?

Children will remember things best when studying with all three modalities (memory channels).[3] One may be a strength. If so, they can start studying with that one, but often using all three enhances their memory more. Like with environmental preferences, you can observe to determine which ones your children prefer. Older children can become self-aware so they can make adjustments to how they practice and study.

Paying attention to modalities is especially relevant when your children need to remember things like spelling words, math facts, vocabulary definitions, and details for tests. They're also relevant when you need children to do chores in a particular order, remember what time to be ready to leave for a party, and how to complete a task. Check out my sample of how to memorize Bible verses with all three modalities at www.StartWithTheHeart.net. You'll be able to use the ideas for math facts, chemistry abbreviations, and any number of other ideas.

Auditory modality—these children remember best the things they hear, especially the things they hear themselves say.

You know you have an auditory child at home if she's constantly talking to herself. If you're homeschooling and you say, "Remember to do only the odd problems today," and your daughter walks away to work mumbling, "Do just the odd problems," that's probably indicative of an auditory child who's figured out on her own that she remembers what she hears herself say.

These children may move their lips while reading silently. This may slow them down, but if they don't do it, they'll most likely remember less. You can encourage them to read out loud and practice studying spelling words by spelling them out loud several times. For auditory children, this is much more effective than having them write them ten times each. They can exaggerate tricky letters. For instance, when spelling s-t-o-r-e, they could whisper or shout the "e" which is silent.

Visual modality—these children remember best the things they see.

To help all children, use the word "study" rather than "look." If you say "Look at the word," your children might wonder why they should when they just wrote it. But when you say "Study the word" they might notice the double consonant. It's fun when I do this in seminars, using "the ceiling." People notice details they didn't see when just looking at it.

Kinesthetic modality—these children remember best the things they do.

Kinesthetic kids are constantly busy with their hands, studying with their fingers. They may count on their fingers and prefer to touch things. For example, your son may remember details about volcanoes when allowed to build one with clay or plaster of Paris. Visual kids will remember details because they watch a DVD or study pictures in books. Auditory children will remember by listening to explanations.

Genius Qualities:
A Strength or A Problem?

When teaching children with learning challenges, Dr. Thomas Armstrong rejected the label of "learning disabled" and simply thought of them as "learning different." The longer he observed, the more he hypothesized that many of these children were probably geniuses. He knew they were bright and could learn, but they frustrated their teachers and were frustrated by school.

Knowing that many classic geniuses had dropped out of school, Dr. Armstrong read their biographies and autobiographies to determine what they had in common. He identified these twelve qualities: curiosity, playfulness, imagination, creativity, wonder, wisdom, inventiveness, vitality, sensitivity, flexibility, humor, and joy.[4]

Do you see any of your children in that list? Many children have one or more of these twelve qualities. Too often, these genius qualities are not valued in school and they can get children into trouble. Children may feel stupid, but tapping into these strengths can change that and increase motivation.

Imagine if you designed assignments, tasks, and chores to honor these qualities as much as possible. Imagine seeing behaviors stemming from these qualities as strengths and not problems. Your children will feel known and appreciated. Children will be more motivated and hopeful. You can encourage children to be curious. They would more naturally seek answers to their questions and look for solutions to problems.[5] These are certainly qualities of self-motivated children.

> **What if children with the quality of wonder were allowed to slow down and think more about some things?**

What if children with the quality of wonder were allowed to slow down and think more about some things? What if children who are imaginative had someone who would listen to their stories and color pictures with them? Imagination has been identified as a survival skill and a key to thriving in the 21st century, as have curiosity and problem-solving.[6] Motivation in the right direction would be more likely. School would be a safer place for them. So would home.

Look for opportunities to celebrate these qualities when you observe them in your children. Talk about the need for self-control so they use them only for good and not to harm. Time management can often be an issue for children with several of these qualities. If that's the case, teach, don't tell and yell. Teach and coach them how to use them while learning, studying, creating, and playing. Keep them alive.

Multiple Intelligences: How Are My Children Smart?

Teaching children how they are smart encourages and inspires them. Some children have wrongly assumed they're not smart because they compared themselves to others who earn better grades. This belief demotivates them. They set lower goals and may pessimistically approach tasks and their future. I've talked with many children who wonder why they should bother studying when they're not smart.

Discovering God created them (and everyone else) with 8 different smarts changes children's identity and can make them more secure in themselves. Using the smarts increases their competence, boosts awareness and confidence in their purpose, and even strengthens friendships. I unpack this in my book *8 Great Smarts* and our Celebrate Kids product line.[7] Here is a description of each of the smarts and a list of various practice methods and assignment formats for each intelligence. Children can learn to listen, practice, and study with the intelligences that are best suited to their assignments and goals. Using the smarts and different formats adds variety to children's learning experiences and increases energy, effort, motivation, and success.

When possible, you can also use children's smarts to assign chores that fit them better than others. For instance, body-smart children may enjoy sweeping out the garage. Logic-smart children may enjoy helping you organize DVDs. Children with nature-smart strengths may enjoy weeding the garden more than other children. These matches can increase obedience and success. And motivation!

Word Smart

When being word smart, children argue, persuade, entertain, and/or instruct effectively through the spoken word. They're often trivia experts. They also tend to be masters of literacy: they read a lot, write clearly, listen intently, and/or speak well. They think with words. When they're excited, they talk and/or write.

Word smart: Read about it, write about it, talk about it, listen to it. Audiotapes, choral readings, class newspapers, diaries, interviews, journals, oral reports, stories, storytelling, read out loud, be expressive, listen to someone read, discuss, debate, vocabulary drills, retype/recopy notes, read related books, lecture, play word games, journal writing, book reports, book commercials, library research, give verbal directions.

Logic Smart

Children reason, sequence, categorize, and think with cause-effects and comparison contrasts when using their logic smart. They think with questions. When they're excited, they ask more questions.

Logic smart: Quantify it, think carefully about it, experiment with it. Calculations, challenges, crossword puzzles, debates, experiments, graphs, objective analyses, predictions, problems to solve, cause-effect thinking, predicting, exploring, self-discovery, use data, use numbers in more than math classes, questions to research, question box on the kitchen table, brain teasers, science experiments, number games, calculators, supply reasons and explanations when they're missing.

Picture Smart

Children who are picture smart are very sensitive to visual details. They can observe, transform, and recreate different aspects of the visual-spatial world. They think in pictures with their eyes. When they're excited, they add to their pictures (in their mind and/or on paper).

Picture smart: See it, examine it, draw it, visualize it, color it, diagram it. Charts, collages, computer graphics, mind maps, observations, picture dictionaries, puzzles, timelines, diagrams, maps, use color on charts, use color often (make all b's blue for a while if a child gets b's and d's confused, highlight main ideas in yellow), ask if answer looks right, dioramas, humor, drama, show and tell, draw definitions of words, practice spelling words/definitions/facts with gel pens on dark paper, field trips, art museums, shapes, geometry, allow time to study things with their eyes, "close your eyes and see."

Music Smart

Hearing, appreciating, and/or producing rhythms and melodies comes easily to children when they use their music smart. They often have a good ear, can sing in tune, keep time to music, and listen to different musical selections with some degree of discernment. They think with rhythms and melodies. When they're excited, they make music.

Music smart: Sing it, rap/rhythm it, listen to it. Cheers, choral readings, cultural music, jingles, Morse code, raps, rhythmic patterns, sound effects, choose songs that fit topic, study the role music played in what you're studying, study music history, read biographies of musicians and composers (excellent way to learn about perseverance and the role of practice), rhyming poetry, use rhythms and melodies to learn things (e.g., Mississippi, the ABC song), read with great expression, clapping math facts.

Body Smart

The evidence of body intelligence can be seen in large motor and/or small motor skills and interests. When being body smart, children can control their body movements and handle objects skillfully. They may enjoy physical pursuits like walking, sports, dancing, acting, or camping and/or they may be skilled at activities like sewing, carpentry, or model building. They think with movement and touch. When they're excited, they move and touch more.

Body smart: Build it, touch it, act it out, get a gut feeling of it, dance it. Charades, costumes, dances, demonstrations, dramas, games, movement, puppet show, role plays, videos, every student response (thumbs up for even answer and thumbs down for odd, stand up when finished, etc.), write at board, clap math facts, manipulatives, time to explore things with their hands, pacing with clipboard, beanbag chairs and rocking chairs in the back of the room, use gestures.

Nature Smart

Children who would rather be outdoors than indoors may be

strong in this smart. They tend to love animals and are knowledgeable about them. When being nature smart, they recognize and classify plants, minerals, and animals. They can also recognize cultural artifacts like cars or sneaker brands. They think with patterns. When they're excited, they go outside, pay attention to plants and animals inside and outside, and make patterns.

Nature smart: Examine it, diagram it, compare it, categorize it, collect it. Animals, collections, conservation, hands-on experiments, nature walks, outside activities, plants, relate topics to nature as often as possible, teach sciences that relate to nature, do experiments involving nature, learn about famous naturalists, compare things based on patterns, categorize and sort things based on similarities and differences, collect data, use magnifiers/microscopes/binoculars/telescopes to study nature, draw or photograph natural objects, study/take breaks outside.

People Smart

Children who are being people smart discern and then respond to the moods, intentions, and desires of others. Therefore, they tend to be leaders. They have the ability (for good or bad) to get inside another person and view the world from that individual's perspective. They think with other people. When they're excited, they talk to people.

People smart: Teach it, collaborate on it, interact with it, use it with others. Communication games, cooperating, discussions, group projects, interviews, peer coaching, sharing, use small groups, assign study groups, use question/answer discussions and ask for students' opinions, ask questions to help them finalize thoughts, give them opportunities to persuade others, use dramatics and excellent facial expression and voice inflection, role play.

Self Smart

Children using this smart know themselves well. They tend to enjoy quiet times of deep soul-searching. They are independent, goal-directed, and self-disciplined. They think with reflection deeply inside of themselves. When they're excited, they spend time alone to reflect more.

Self smart: Think deeply about it, connect it to your life, make choices about it. Autobiographies, diaries, impersonations, journals, learning logs, observations, opinions, reflections, let them learn and study alone when possible, give them time to think deeply (three minutes in class and overnight for deeper thinking), give them time to explain their ideas, give choices, use self-paced projects, use individualized instruction, connect topics to personal lives, say things like "close your eyes and think of a time when . . ."

WHAT ABOUT YOU?

Thinking back to when you were in school, what difference would it have made if you knew how you learn best? Can you think of times you would have been more motivated and more successful? What about now? Did you learn anything about yourself here? Might some changes because of your environmental preferences improve your quiet time and learning? Would a different use of modalities enhance Bible verse memorization? What else?

THINGS TO DO

- Observe your children when they're able to concentrate and when they're not. Ask them if they're aware of their environment and what might be contributing to their successes and struggles. Discuss changes and get your children's agreement.

- Have your children try memorizing something with the three modalities and try to determine which might be a current strength. Ask your children if they know what works best for them. Tell them what you noticed. (Remember the sample on the website. The examples will help you.)

- Show the descriptions of the eight smarts to your children. Enjoy sharing examples of how each member in your family is smart. Try to list the top four for each person.

- Go to this book's website, www.StartWithTheHeart.net, to find a list of study strategy categories and suggestions for teaching study strategies. These thoughts may be relevant if you believe your children want to do well, but need help with study strategies.

THINGS TO THINK ABOUT

- Which of the genius qualities do you value? How can you encourage your children to use those in healthy and wise ways?

- Which content related to the eight smarts might your children enjoy learning about? Artists? Soccer rules? History of their favorite words? Names of trees in your neighborhood?

Keep hold of instruction; do not let go;
guard her, for she is your life.

PROVERBS 4:13

AND FINALLY . . .

How are you feeling? Energized? Overwhelmed? Hopeful?

I have given you a *lot* of information, I know. Hopefully you've applied ideas as you've been reading and you're encouraged. Now, it may be helpful to skim back through the book, focusing on areas that are especially relevant to you and the child you're most concerned about so you can think about more insights and apply more ideas. But whatever your challenges are, and whatever "smarts" your children possess, remember this: in all the little moments, with so many choices to make and actions to take, it really gets down to this one thing: the heart! Your child's heart. Always . . . start with the heart.

APPENDIX A

Character Qualities

Attentive	Dedicated	Generous
Authentic	Dependable	Gentle
Bold	Determined	Grateful
Brave	Devoted	Honest
Caring	Diligent	Hopeful
Cautious	Discerning	Hospitable
Cheerful	Discrete	Humble
Committed	Effort	Integrity
Compassionate	Endurance	Joyful
Confident	Enthusiastic	Kind
Consistent	Fair	Loving
Content	Faithful	Loyal
Cooperative	Flexible	Meek
Courageous	Forgiving	Merciful
Decisive	Friendly	Obedient

Optimistic	Resourceful	Thankful
Passionate	Respectful	Thoughtful
Patient	Responsible	Thrifty
Peaceful	Righteous	Tolerant
Persevering	Self-Controlled	Trustworthy
Persuasive	Self-Disciplined	Truthful
Polite	Sensitive	Unselfish
Punctual	Servant	Vulnerable
Pure	Sincere	Wise
Repentant	Teachable	

How to Teach Character
(by Steve and Joyce Baker)[1]

Parents want their children to grow and mature into responsible, brave, and compassionate adults—people of character. Yet a great deal of parent's energy is spent on behavioral management rather than the objective. Outward behavior is based upon inward character, so heart transformation is the necessary ideal in parenting.

Four practical ways to do this can be found in the life of Jesus as He nurtured, taught, and trained the disciples: Imitation, Intentionality, Individuality, and Intensity.

TEACH BY IMITATION

Jesus encouraged those who followed Him to "take my yoke upon you, and learn from me" (Matthew 11:29). He was encouraging the disciples to imitate Him in the same way He imitated His Father (John 5). Children naturally begin to talk and walk like their parents. As your children's first role models, work to imitate Christ in behavior and conversation so you can encourage them to imitate you.

Children benefit from seeing your purposeful imitation of Jesus Christ and the boundaries you set for yourself. They must see your dependence on God and your repentance, sacrifice, humility, honesty, and compassion lived out day by day in failure or success. No doubt, you will both fail and succeed, but you build a boundary of security around your children when they see your genuine dependence on God and love for Jesus. Because it's about God, they won't experience this boundary as a wall of behavioral regulations they can hardly wait to scale and escape.

TEACH INTENTIONALLY

Imitation leads to intentionality. Psalm 127:3–4 reminds us that "children are a heritage from the LORD, the fruit of the womb a reward. Like arrows in the hand of a warrior are the children of one's youth." God designed children and has a plan for them. Your goal can not be to raise them to be who you want them to be. It should not even be to raise them to be who they want to be. Your intentional goal should be to help them develop into the people God designed them to be.

TEACH INDIVIDUALLY

Part of intentional parenting is recognizing individuality because each one of your children is completely different. Psalm 139 clearly reveals God made us and knows us individually. You cannot demand that siblings share the same interests or expect them to have all the same abilities. Each child thinks differently, communicates differently, and shows different love and response to correction. In order to furnish a secure place for their identity to develop, we must recognize those differences and provide discipline and encouragement accordingly.

Teach your children to gratefully embrace the individual God created them to be. Jesus dealt with Peter in John 21 differently than all the other disciples, and He encouraged him not to worry about God's plans for the others. His discipline was personal and challenging. Jesus treated everyone as an individual.

TEACH WITH INTENSITY

All of the intentional individuality and imitation will be limited in influence to your children if it does not have a corresponding level of intensity. Passion is caught more than it is taught. Numerous parents have taught their children the correct ideals and doctrines of their faith. They have taken them to church and had some form of family devotions. They say it's all very important.

However, as these children observe their parents, they clearly *see* their parents' true passion. What they observe could validate and reinforce their faith confession or it could cause a conflict in the child's spirit. Are actions contradicting their parents' words? Enjoying sports, business, travel, and other pursuits is fine, but keep God as the passion of your life. Intentionally invest in God's kingdom with your time, energy, finances, and fun.

Disciple-making is the character development we are seeking to accomplish in our children by our intense, intentional, and individual imitation of Christ.

Parker's Complete Vision Statement[1]

Parker

OUR VISION

"More alike than different." Parker is more like his peers than he is different. He will learn to do everything his typical peers can do; it just might take a bit longer. Our goal for Parker this year is to become acclimated to the learning environment and to grow to love it. We want him to work on developing relationships with his peers and to learn appropriate behaviors for social settings. Our long-term goal is for Parker to be happy and learn to be an independent adult who contributes to the community in which he lives.

THINGS TO KNOW
Parker is a smart, strong-willed little boy who is very open to learning. He loves to learn new things and gets very excited when he does. He loves receiving praise when he accomplishes a task. Parker oftentimes watches his peers before joining in on a task. He is a very visual learner. Although his expressive language is still emerging, his receptive understanding of his surroundings is fantastic. He will get distracted if spending too much time on each task and will need redirection. If he is asked to do something he isn't interested in, he will become frustrated. In this situation, redirection works well.

FAVORITE THINGS
- Music and dancing
- Books
- Giving hugs
- Donuts
- Bubble Guppies
- Mickey Mouse
- Running and moving
- Laughing and being funny

WORKING ON . . .

- Fine motor skills
- Expressive language
- Staying on task
- Not running off
- Drinking from open cup

WHAT WORKS

- Redirection
- Praise/positive reinforcement
- Sign language
- Modeling/visuals
- Demonstrating
- Offering two choices
- Explaining what is happening

WHAT DOESN'T

- Negative reinforcement
- Multi-directional tasks
- Stationary learning
- Spending too much time on each task
- Rushing

What Seventh Graders Said about Identity

These are descriptive words four hundred seventh graders listed, while working in small groups, to describe their ideal identity in the six categories I taught them about. What words would you love your kids to list?

INTELLECTUAL IDENTITY

smart, doing well in school, musically gifted, creative, learns quickly, talented, intelligent, artistic, unique, processing, history, bugs, science, robotics, original thinker, wise beyond their years, focused, motivated

EMOTIONAL IDENTITY

loving, caring, stable, kind, friendly, joyful, happy, compassionate, resilient, grateful, kind-hearted, humble, mature, trustworthy, optimistic, in control of emotions

SOCIAL IDENTITY

teamwork, outspoken, friendly, nice, helpful, people like being around me, outgoing, a lot of friends, interactive, open, trustworthy, compassionate, fun to be around, respectful, perky, responsible, funny, kind, optimistic, caring, optimistically outgoing, good at talking to people, self-control, easy to get along with

CHARACTER IDENTITY

kind, encouraging, trustworthy, charismatic, good, honest, truthful, sweet, loyal, integrity, perky, always happy, bubbly, friendly, peppy, humble, helpful, careful, loving, compassionate, loyal, respectful, easygoing, positive, problem solver, open-minded, hardworking, diligent, responsible, courageous, good role model

PHYSICAL IDENTITY

strong, athletic, fast, good-looking, beautiful, sexy, pretty, in shape, good at sports, handsome, muscular, physically fit, diverse, beautiful in their own way, comfortable, different, unique, comfortable with yourself, confident, naturally healthy

SPIRITUAL IDENTITY

be a good Christian with actions, peace, close to God, godly man, teachable, on the right path, loving, Christ follower, faithful, disciple maker, missionary, the hands and feet of Christ, Christian, faithful, believer, passionate, bright from the inside, have a strong faith in God, close to God, heart for Christ

Complimenting Words

Able to . . .	Caring	Disciplined
Accurate	Cautious	Discreet
Alert	Cheerful	Dynamic
Ambitious	Clever	Eager
Analytical	Compassionate	Efficient
Appreciative	Complete	Empathetic
Articulate	Confident	Encouraging
Assertive	Conscientious	Energetic
Attentive	Consistent	Enthusiastic
Available	Creative	Ethical
Aware	Curious	Fair
Becoming . . .	Decisive	Faithful
Bold	Dependable	Flexible
Brave	Determined	Focused
Calm	Diligent	Forgiving
Careful	Discerning	Friendly

Fun	Inspiring	Perceptive
Generous	Interesting	Persevering
Gentle	Intuitive	Persuasive
Genuine	Inventive	Planner
Goal setter	Joyful	Pleasant
Good example	Kind	Polite
Good follower	Knowledgeable	Positive
Good listener	Leader	Precise
Good sport	Learning to . . .	Problem solver
Gracious	Likable	Punctual
Grateful	Logical	Quick
Hard-working	Loving	Reasonable
Healthy	Loyal	Relaxed
Helpful	Mature	Reliable
Honest	Merry	Resilient
Hopeful	Motivated	Resourceful
Hospitable	Neat	Respectful
Humble	Nice	Responsible
Humorous	Obedient	Secure
Imaginative	Open-minded	Self-controlled
Improving	Optimistic	Sensible
Independent	Organized	Sensitive
Ingenious	Others-centered	Service-minded
Innovative	Patient	Shares well
Insightful	Peaceful	Sincere

Smart

Spirited

Spontaneous

Stable

Steadfast

Strong

Successful

Tactful

Teachable

Tender-hearted

Thorough

Thoughtful

Thrifty

Tolerant

Trusting

Trustworthy

Understanding

Unselfish

Unique

Wise

Wise choices

Correcting Words

Aggressive	Clumsy	Distracting
Agitated	Controlling	Domineering
Angry	Deceptive	Egotistical
Anxious	Defiant	Envious
Apathetic	Demanding	Erratic
Argumentative	Dependent	Exaggerated
Arrogant	Depressed	Exhausted
Bad example	Despairing	Fake
Bitter	Disagreeable	Fearful
Boastful	Discouraging	Fidgety
Boring	Disheartened	Foolish
Brash	Dishonest	Fussy
Bullied	Disobedient	Gives up easily
Callous	Disorganized	Gloomy
Careless	Disrespectful	Gossiping
Closed-minded	Disruptive	Hard-hearted

Harmful	Interrupted	Overcautious
Harsh	Intolerant	Overconfident
Hateful	Irrational	Overwhelmed
Hesitant	Irrelevant	Passive
Hot-headed	Irresponsible	Pessimistic
Humorless	Irreverent	Poor sport
Hurried	Irritating	Prejudiced
Hurtful	Joyless	Presumptuous
Hypocritical	Judging	Pretending
Idle	Lack initiative	Proud
Ignorant	Lack integrity	Quarrelsome
Illogical	Late	Reckless
Immature	Lazy	Rejecting
Impatient	Manipulative	Resistant
Impolite	Materialistic	Restless
Impractical	Mean	Rude
Impulsive	Meddlesome	Sarcastic
Inattentive	Mischievous	Satisfied
Incomplete	Miserable	Self-indulgent
Inconsiderate	Negative	Selfish
Inconsistent	Nervous	Silent
Indifferent	Nosy	Silly
Inflexible	Obstinate	Slanderous
Insecure	Offensive	Slick
Insincere	Oppressive	Sloppy

Slow

Sly

Smart aleck

Spiteful

Spontaneous

Stagnant

Stingy

Stuck

Suspicious

Tactless

Tardy

Teased

Tense

Timid

Unable to . . .

Unaccountable

Unavailable

Unaware

Uncaring

Uncomfortable

Uncommitted

Unconcerned

Undependable

Underachiever

Undisciplined

Unenthusiastic

Unethical

Unfair

Unfaithful

Unfeeling

Unfocused

Unfriendly

Unhappy

Unhealthy

Unimaginative

Unjust

Unkind

Unknowing

Unloving

Unmotivated

Unpleasant

Unpredictable

Unrealistic

Unreasonable

Unreliable

Unresponsive

Unruly

Unsafe

Unstable

Unsuccessful

Unwilling

Violent

Wasteful

Weak

Weary

Wrong

Acknowledgments

My brother and I were celebrated. Our parents naturally motivated us well and, in addition to prioritizing our academics, we were involved in athletics, music, outside-of-school activities, church, and family activities. I am very grateful for my upbringing. I was blessed to be well supported by my parents and extended family. Oh, how I wish each child could say the same!

When I taught second graders, motivating students wasn't as easy as I assumed it would be. Some appeared afraid to try. Some who were very capable, weren't interested in pushing themselves. They, their parents, and my colleagues fueled my early interests in motivation and related topics. I'm thankful.

Professors at Purdue University taught and motivated me well. Realizing how much of my PhD studies in educational psychology came back to me as I wrote this book was inspiring. I had many excellent teachers from kindergarten through graduate school. I'm thankful.

Brad Sargent transcribed several of my messages and that helped as I began this book. He also helped create the appendixes of correcting and complimenting words. He has been a

274   START WITH THE HEART

trusted friend and colleague for twenty-five years. Amy Tracy was a trusted consultant on ideas and my writing. Many Facebook friends answered questions I posted and helped me develop ideas. I'm thankful.

Nancy Matheis, our Project Manager, also improved this book with her important reactions and insights. Linda Depler and Debbie Thompson, my assistants, managed the office well so I didn't need to be concerned with certain things while writing. Tina Hollenbeck continues to write valuable columns for the Celebrate Kids email newsletter. Meg Hykes put up with my crazy schedule as our social media manager. Gloria Leyda, my agent at Ambassadors Speakers Bureau, continues to work hard to get me speaking events so I can influence parents, teachers, and kids of all ages. Many people at Moody Publishers believe in me and worked with me to create this readable and beneficial book. They all serve the Lord and me beautifully and sacrificially. I'm thankful.

The emotional investment, prayer support, and wisdom of my Board of Directors is always essential. Colleagues Mary Margaret Gibson, Lane Phillips, and Suzanne Phillips provided tremendous emotional support. Without them and my family, church family, and numerous other friends, I couldn't accomplish what I do. I'm thankful.

I'm grateful to God for His grace and for compelling me to want much out of life. He is why I am who I am and why I do what I do.

Notes

Chapter 1: Relationships Rule

1. Tedd Tripp, *Shepherding a Child's Heart* (Wapwallopen, PA: Shepherd Press, 1995), 96.
2. Lori Wildenberg, *The Messy Life of Parenting: Powerful and Practical Ways to Strengthen Family Connections* (Birmingham, AL: New Hope Publishers, 2018), 10.
3. Karen Reivich and Andrew Shatte, *The Resilience Factor: 7 Keys to Finding Your Inner Strength and Overcoming Life's Hurdles* (New York: Broadway Books, 2003).
4. Mayo Clinic Staff, "Resilience: Build Skills to Endure Hardship," Mayo Clinic, May 18, 2017, https://www.mayoclinic.org/tests-procedures/resilience-training/in-depth/resilience/art-20046311.
5. Ibid.
6. Ibid.
7. Debbie Silver and Dedra Stafford, *Teaching Kids to Thrive: Essential Skills for Success* (Thousand Oaks, CA: Corwin, 2017).
8. Ibid.
9. https://www.marquette.edu/universityhonors/speakers-rogers.shtml.

Chapter 2: Character: A Skill and A Will

1. Michael A. Zigarelli, *Cultivating Christian Character: How to Become the Person God Wants You to Be and How to Help Others Do the Same* (Colorado Springs: Purposeful Design, 2005).
2. Jill Savage and I include a lengthy appendix of a hundred character qualities, including definitions, in our book: *No More Perfect Kids: Love Your Kids for Who They Are* (Chicago: Moody, 2013), 233–41.
3. Thomas Lickona, *How to Raise Kind Kids and Get Respect, Gratitude, and a Happier Family in the Bargain* (New York: Penguin Books, 2018), 83.
4. Roy F. Baumeister and John Tierney, *Willpower: Rediscovering the Greatest Human Strength* (New York: Penguin Books, 2012).

5. Debbie Silver and Dedra Stafford, *Teaching Kids to Thrive: Essential Skills for Success* (Thousand Oaks, CA: Corwin, 2017), 53–54.
6. Lori Wildenberg, *The Messy Life of Parenting: Powerful and Practical Ways to Strengthen Family Connections* (Birmingham, AL: New Hope Publishers, 2018), 13.
7. Tony Wagner, *The Global Achievement Gap: Why Even Our Best Schools Don't Teach the New Survival Skills Our Children Need—and What We Can Do About It* (New York: Basic Books, 2008). See also Tony Wagner, "Rigor Redefined," *Educational Leadership* 66, no. 2 (2008): 20–25.
8. Debbie Silver and Dedra Stafford, *Teaching Kids to Thrive: Essential Skills for Success* (Thousand Oaks, CA: Corwin, 2017), 129.
9. Ibid., 165.
10. Ibid., 88.
11. Ibid., 165.
12. Attributed to Samuel Smiles on Goodreads, https://www.goodreads.com/quotes/272583-sow-a-thought-and-you-reap-an-act-sow-an; however, see "Watch Your Thoughts, They Become Words; Watch Your Words, They Become Actions," Quote Investigator, https://quoteinvestigator.com/2013/01/10/watch-your-thoughts/.

Chapter 3: What Makes Change Happen?

1. Gayle Gregory and Martha Kaufeldt, *The Motivated Brain: Improving Student Attention, Engagement, and Perseverance* (Alexandria, VA: ASCD, 2015), 9.
2. Colossians 3:1–17—If then you have been raised with Christ, seek the things that are above, where Christ is, seated at the right hand of God. Set your minds on things that are above, not on things that are on earth. For you have died, and your life is hidden with Christ in God. When Christ who is your life appears, then you also will appear with him in glory.

Put to death therefore what is earthly in you: sexual immorality, impurity, passion, evil desire, and covetousness, which is idolatry. On account of these the wrath of God is coming. In these you too once walked, when you were living in them. But now you must put them all away: anger, wrath, malice, slander, and obscene talk from your mouth. Do not lie to one another, seeing that you have put off the old self with its practices and have put on the new self, which is being renewed in knowledge after the image of its creator. Here there is not Greek and Jew, circumcised and uncircumcised, barbarian, Scytian, slave, free; but Christ is all, and in all.

Put on then, as God's chosen ones, holy and beloved, compassionate hearts, kindness, humility, meekness, and patience, bearing with one another and, if one has a complaint against another, forgiving each other; as the Lord has forgiven you, so you also must forgive. And above all these put on love, which binds everything together in perfect harmony. And let the peace of Christ rule in your hearts, to which indeed you were called in one body. And be thankful. Let the word of Christ dwell in you richly, teaching and admonishing one another in all wisdom, singing psalms and hymns and spiritual songs, with thankfulness in your hearts to God. And whatever you do, in word or deed, do everything in the name of the Lord Jesus, giving thanks to God the Father through him.

3. For example, when I examined reasons I interrupted, partly for chapter 5 in *Finding Authentic Hope and Wholeness,* I realized I did it because I quickly come up with ideas as I listen, I believe ideas are important, and I want to encourage people by providing solutions. These things are easy for me to do because of my training as an educator, my gift of teaching, and my spiritual gift of exhortation. That doesn't make interrupting right. That's a key! Even good causes are wrong when they contribute to wrong behavior. It's rare that we only have good causes. I also discovered I interrupted because I thought my ideas were more important than theirs, I didn't think they would come up with my ideas, and talking gets me more attention than listening. Ouch!

4. Robin Sharma, Twitter post, April 8, 2014, 3:00 a.m., https://twitter.com/RobinSharma/status/453472361421877248.

5. Kathy Koch, *Screens and Teens: Connecting with Our Kids in a Wireless World* (Chicago: Moody Publishers, 2015), 113.

6. Ibid.

7. Scotty Smith, *Everyday Prayers: 365 Days to a Gospel-Centered Faith* (Grand Rapids: Baker Books, 2011), 193.

Chapter 4: The Five Core Needs

1. Tedd Tripp, *Shepherding a Child's Heart* (Wapwallopen, PA: Shepherd Press, 1995), page xviii.

2. These core needs, especially the Biblical applications of them, are explained in detail in my book *Finding Authentic Hope and Wholeness: Five Questions That Will Change Your Life* (Chicago: Moody Publishers, 2005). Bible verses relevant to how God meets each need are listed on the book's website: www.AuthenticHope.com.

3. Daniel Pink, *Drive: The Surprising Truth About What Motivates Us* (New York: Riverhead Books, 2009).

4. Kathy Koch, *Screens and Teens: Connecting with Our Kids in a Wireless World* (Chicago: Moody, 2015), 90.

5. Jennifer Fredericks, *Eight Myths of Student Disengagement: Creating Classrooms of Deep Learning* (Thousand Oaks, CA: Corwin, 2014).

6. William Glasser, *Choice Theory: A New Psychology of Personal Freedom* (New York: Harper Collins, 1998).

7. Gayle Gregory and Martha Kaufeldt, *The Motivated Brain: Improving Student Attention, Engagement, and Perseverance* (Alexandria, VA: ASCD, 2015), 125.

8. Nina Godlewski, "Mr. Rogers Quotes: Wisdom From the Children's Television Host on His Birthday," *Newsweek*, March 20, 2018, https://www.newsweek.com/fred-rogers-birthday-quotes-wont-you-be-my-neighbor-movie-854013.

Chapter 5: Believe It!—and Thrive

1. Deborah Stipek, *Motivation to Learn: From Theory to Practice*, 2nd ed. (Boston: Allyn and Bacon, 1993). See also Raymond Wlodkowski and Judith Jaynes, *Eager to Learn: Helping Children Become Motivated and Love Learning* (San Francisco: Jossey-Bass Publishers, 1990). Other reading and numerous observations and conversations solidified my thinking about these three beliefs.
2. Arun Pradhan, "Infographic: 3 Facts about Mindset in Learning," *The Learnnovators* (blog), November 16, 2015, https://learnnovators.com/blog/infographic-3-facts-about-mindset-in-learning/.
3. Facebook post and personal communication, September 2, 2018.
4. Kathy Koch, *Screens and Teens: Connecting with Our Kids in a Wireless World* (Chicago: Moody, 2015).
5. "Martha Graham Quotes," BrainyQuote.com, https://www.brainyquote.com/quotes/martha_graham_140937, accessed October 25, 2018.

Chapter 6: You—a Coach?

1. Angela Duckworth, *Grit: The Power of Passion and Perseverance* (London, England: Vermilion, 2016), 212.
2. Ibid., 200.
3. John Watson, quoted in ibid.
4. Ibid.
5. Tedd Tripp, *Shepherding a Child's Heart* (Wapwallopen, PA: Shepherd Press, 1995), 38.
6. Alfie Kohn, *Punished By Rewards: The Trouble with Gold Stars, Incentive Plans, A's, Praise, and Other Bribes* (New York: Houghton Mifflin, 1999).
7. Edward Deci, Richard Koestner, and Richard Ryan, "A Meta-Analytic Review of Experiments Examining the Effects of Extrinsic Rewards on Intrinsic Motivation," *Psychological Bulletin* 125, no. 6 (1999): 627–68.

Chapter 7: How to Communicate So Your Children Will Hear You

1. Karen Reivich and Andrew Shatte, *The Resilience Factor: 7 Keys to Finding Your Inner Strength and Overcoming Life's Hurdles* (New York: Broadway Books, 2003).
2. Watty Piper, *The Little Engine That Could* (New York: Platt & Munk Publishers, 1930).
3. Debbie Silver and Dedra Stafford, *Teaching Kids to Thrive: Essential Skills for Success* (Thousand Oaks, CA: Corwin, 2017), 135–36.

Chapter 8: Listening Longer and Other Essentials of Good Communication

1. Lee David Daniels, *Grit for Kids: 16 Top Steps for Developing Grit, Passion, Willpower, and Perseverance in Kids for Self-Confidence and a Successful Life* (self pub., 2016).

2. I address this in detail, with my coauthor Jill Savage, in *No More Perfect Kids: Love Your Kids for Who They Are* (Chicago: Moody, 2013).
3. Mike Fabarez, *Raising Men, Not Boys: Shepherding Your Sons to be Men of God.* (Chicago: Moody Publishers, 2017). See also, Steve Gerali, *Teenage Guys: Exploring Issues Adolescent Guys Face and Strategies to Help Them* (Grand Rapids, MI: Zondervan, 2006). See also, Susan Morris Shaffer and Linda Perlman Gordon, *Why Boys Don't Talk and Why it Matters: A Parent's Survival Guide to Connecting with Your Teen* (New York: McGraw-Hill. 2005).

Chapter 9: Complimenting and Correcting

1. I've simplified things by often using www.dictionary.com for the definitions included in this book. But, I do have huge dictionaries, including a Webster's International Dictionary of the English Language from 1909 that comprises updated versions of the first editions from 1864, 1879, and 1884 that I enjoy using. It's one of my prized possessions. I also own and use my two volumes of the *New Shorter Oxford English Dictionary* (volume 1: A-M, volume 2: N-Z).
2. James Hamblin, "100 Percent Is Overrated," *The Atlantic*, June 30, 2015, https://www.theatlantic.com/education/archive/2015/06/the-s-word/397205/. See also Salman Khan, "The Learning Myth: Why I'll Never Tell My Son He's Smart," *Huffington Post*, August 19, 2014, https://www.huffingtonpost.com/salman-khan/the-learning-myth-why-ill_b_5691681.html. See also Headmistress/Zookeeper, "Don't Tell Your Kids They're Smart," *The Common Room* (blog), September 25, 2013, http://thecommonroomblog.com/2013/09/dont-tell-your-kids-theyre-smart.html. See also Alexandra Ossola, "Too Many Kids Quit Science Because They Don't Think They're Smart," *The Atlantic*, November 3, 2014, https://www.theatlantic.com/education/archive/2014/11/too-many-kids-quit-science-because-they-dont-think-theyre-smart/382165/.
3. Carol Dweck, *Mindset: The New Psychology of Success* (New York: Ballantine Books, 2007).
4. Karen Reivich and Andrew Shatte, *The Resilience Factor: 7 Keys to Finding Your Inner Strength and Overcoming Life's Hurdles* (New York: Broadway Books, 2003).
5. I elaborate on what these six identities are and how and why to provide feedback to all of them in chapter 4 of *Finding Authentic Hope and Wholeness: Five Questions that Will Change Your Life*. Also, Lori Wildenberg's *101 Affirmations to Bless Your Child's Heart* are wonderful in *The Messy Life of Parenting* (Birmingham, AL: New Hope Publishers, 2018), 167–70.
6. Because identity controls behavior and you want to be most intentional about their spiritual development, check out the spiritual identity statements at http://celebratekids.com/authentichope/chapter-four-identity/#relatedscriptures.

7. Kathy Koch, *Screens and Teens: Connecting with Our Kids in a Wireless World* (Chicago: Moody, 2015).
8. Anthony Gregorc, *An Adult's Guide to Style* (Hartford, CT: Gregorc and Associates, 1986).

Chapter 10: You *Can* Help Your Child Learn

1. Gayle Gregory and Martha Kaufeldt, *The Motivated Brain: Improving Student Attention, Engagement, and Perseverance* (Alexandria, VA: ASCD, 2015), 53. See also Merrill Harmin and Melanie Toth, *Inspiring Active Learning: A Complete Handbook for Today's Teachers* (Alexandria, VA: ASCD, 2007).
2. Rita Dunn and Kenneth Dunn, *Teaching Secondary Students Through Their Individual Learning Styles: Practical Approaches for Grades 7–12* (Boston: Allyn & Bacon,1993). See also Rita Dunn, Kenneth Dunn, and Janet Perrin, *Teaching Young Children Through Their Individual Learning Styles: Practical Approaches for Grades K–2*. (New York: St. John's University, 1993).
3. Walter Barbe and Raymond H. Swassing, *Teaching Through Modality Strengths: Concepts and Practices* (Columbus: Zaner-Bloser, Inc., 1979).
4. Thomas Armstrong, *Awakening Genius in the Classroom* (Alexandria, VA: ASCD, 1998), 3–14. See also the book I wrote with two colleagues. We include how to keep the qualities alive and what shuts them down. Kathy Koch, Tina Hollenbeck, and Brad Sargent, *Celebrating Children's 12 Genius Qualities* (Fort Worth, TX: Celebrate Kids, Inc., 2014), https://shop.celebratekids.com/books/celebrating-childrens-12-genius-qualities/.
5. Gayle Gregory and Martha Kaufeldt, *The Motivated Brain: Improving Student Attention, Engagement, and Perseverance* (Alexandria, VA: ASCD, 2015), 54.
6. Tony Wagner, *The Global Achievement Gap: Why Even Our Best Schools Don't Teach the New Survival Skills Our Children Need—and What We Can Do About It* (New York: Basic Books, 2008), 51–57. See also Tony Wagner, "Rigor Redefined," *Educational Leadership* 66, no. 2 (2008): 20–25.
7. My book *8 Great Smarts: Discover and Nurture Your Child's Intelligences* (Chicago: Moody Publishers, 2016) explains these in great detail. You can find a list of other products in the smarts product line on our website here: https://shop.celebratekids.com/8-great-smarts/.

Appendix B: How to Teach Character

1. Used by permission.

Appendix C: Parker's Complete Vision Statement

1. Used by permission.

ABOUT KATHY KOCH, PhD,
and Celebrate Kids, Inc.

Dr. Kathy Koch ("cook"), the founder and president of Celebrate Kids, Inc., has influenced thousands of parents, teachers, teens, and children in 30 countries through keynote messages, seminars, banquets, chapels, and other events.

Dr. Kathy is a featured speaker for the Great Homeschool Conventions and a regular presenter for Care Net, Summit Ministries, and other organizations. She speaks regularly at schools, churches, and pregnancy resource centers. She is also a popular guest on Focus on the Family radio and other radio talk-shows. Kirk Cameron chose her as the technology expert to interview in his 2018 movie, *Connect: Real Help for Parenting Kids in a Social Media World*. This is her sixth book. Her others include *Screens and Teens* and *8 Great Smarts*.

Celebrate Kids renews and revitalizes families by empowering parents and children to meaningfully connect by helping them meet their five core needs in healthy ways and through other compelling reasons, valuable truths, and engaging methods so they value their family unit and are known there, wanted there, and able to establish strong, rooted relationships.

Through presentations in conventions, churches, schools, and for organizations; online, live, and on-demand seminars; an extensive product line; our social media presence; and our bi-weekly email newsletter, Celebrate Kids offers authentic hope for today and tomorrow and relevant solutions that work.

Dr. Kathy Koch founded Celebrate Kids in 1991, after serving as an elementary teacher, middle school coach, school board member, and university professor. Originally from Wauwatosa, a Milwaukee, WI, suburb, she moved to Fort Worth, TX, from Green Bay, WI, to fulfill God's purposes for her.

Website and Blog: www.CelebrateKids.com

Website for this book: www.StartWithTheHeart.net

Video: www.vimeo.com/channels/kathyisms

Facebook: www.facebook.com/celebratekidsinc

Pinterest: www.pinterest.com/kathycelebrate/

Instagram: www.instagram.com/celebratekidskathykoch/

Twitter: @DrKathyKoch

YOUR CHILD IS SMART, BUT DOES HE OR SHE *BELIEVE* IT?

IF YOU FEEL LIKE YOU'RE LOSING YOUR TEEN TO TECHNOLOGY, YOU'RE NOT ALONE.

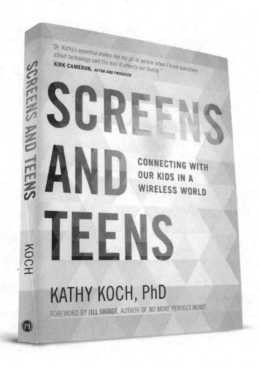